Praise for PowerShift

"*PowerShift* changes the way you think about yourself, your career, and the way you are living. This book gives you a proven framework to live aligned with your true priorities and by doing so, you'll unleash more achievement and joy."
　　—**TIA GRAHAM,** Keynote Speaker, Bestselling Author, and Founder of The Feel Good Club

"In *PowerShift*, Gia Lacqua offers a wake-up call for every woman who's ever felt crushed under the weight of "having it all." With honesty, insight, and wisdom, Gia challenges the myth of balance and instead shows us how to pursue what truly matters with strategy, intention, and self-compassion. *PowerShift* is both a mirror and a road map, a deeply relatable guide to stop proving and start choosing. Every modern woman needs this book on her nightstand!"
　　—**TARA CLARK,** Author of *Modern Mom Probs: A Survival Guide for 21st Century Mothers*

"*PowerShift* is a refreshing reminder that success isn't about doing more—it's about aligning with what truly matters. Gia gives high-achieving women permission to stop chasing balance and start building a life that feels as good as it looks."
　　—**BARB BETTS,** CEO, Keynote Speaker, Podcast Host, and Author of *The Relationship Advantage*

"*PowerShift* names the real cost of 'doing it all' and gives women a smarter way forward. The framework builds clarity, protects capacity, and turns scattered effort into focused results. Every high-achieving woman should read this."
　　—**GARRETT WOOD,** NBC-HWC, CCHt and Founder of Gnosis Therapy

"*PowerShift* is the wake-up call every ambitious woman needs. Gia Lacqua reminds us that real success isn't about doing more, it's about doing what truly matters. This book is equal parts inspiration and roadmap."
—**SIMONE KNEGO,** Women's Leadership Speaker and Author of *REAL Confidence: A Simple Guide to Go from Unsure to Unshakeable*

"*PowerShift* is a revelation for every woman who has ever been told to chase success at the expense of herself. Gia Lacqua reminds us that high-achieving women aren't just ambitious—they're survivors. Her guided exercises offer a transformative path to wholeness, purpose, and self-defined power. This is more than a book; it's an awakening to the woman you were always meant to be."
—**SHANNA JAFRI,** Nonprofit Board Chair and Advocate for Women's Leadership

POWERSHIFT

POWERSHIFT

From Balancing It All
to the Strategic Pursuit of
WHAT MATTERS MOST

gia lacqua

PowerShift: From Balancing It All to the Strategic Pursuit of What Matters Most

Copyright © 2026 by Gia Lacqua

All rights reserved. No part of this publication may be reproduced, stored in a retrieval system, or transmitted in any form by any means, electronic, mechanical, photocopy, recording, or otherwise, without the prior permission of the publisher, except as provided by USA copyright law.

No patent liability is assumed with respect to the use of the information contained herein. Although every precaution has been taken in the preparation of this book, the publisher and author assume no responsibility for errors or omissions. Neither is any liability assumed for damages resulting from the use of the information contained herein.

This book is a work of nonfiction. Names and identifying details have been changed in some cases to protect the privacy of individuals.

Radical Prioritization® is now a registered trademark of Gia Lacqua and may not be used without permission.

Unless otherwise noted, all statistics are from "The Quiet Crisis" white paper by Gia Lacqua and available at https://gialacqua.com/research.

For permission requests, speaking inquiries, or bulk purchases, please contact: empower@gialacqua.com

Published by Mission Driven Press, an imprint of Forefront Books, Nashville, Tennessee. Distributed by Simon & Schuster.

Library of Congress Control Number: 2025921548

Print ISBN: 978-1-63763-481-3

E-book ISBN: 978-1-63763-482-0

Cover Design by George Stevens, G Sharp Design LLC
Interior Design by Bill Kersey, KerseyGraphics

Printed in the United States of America

26 27 28 29 30 31 [RR4] 10 9 8 7 6 5 4 3 2 1

DEDICATION

*To every woman who's ever questioned her worth
while carrying the weight of the world—*

This book is for you.

*For the ones who kept it all together while falling apart inside.
For the ones who achieved everything they were told to want—and
still felt empty.
For the ones who were labeled "too much," "too ambitious," or "too emotional"—and tried to shrink to fit.*

*You're not broken. You've just outgrown the
version of you that was built to survive.*

*May these pages help you remember the truth you've
always known but were conditioned to ignore: You
don't have to prove. You get to choose.*

*Here's to your PowerShift.
Because when you lead from alignment, your world
changes—and so does everyone else's.*

CONTENTS

Author's Note..11
Introduction 13

PART I:
Shift Happens When You're Done Settling

Chapter 1: The Masks We Wear—and Why They're Suffocating You 21
Chapter 2: She's Running the Show—but She's Not You.................35
Chapter 3: The Cost of Carrying It All 47
Chapter 4: The Never-Enough Cycle—How You Got Here and Why
    It's Breaking You..63

PART II:
Radical Prioritization: Identity First. Strategy Second.

Chapter 5: Radical Prioritization: The Shift That Changes Everything....85
Chapter 6: How Identity Shapes Your World, Your Choices, and Your
    Outcomes..99
Chapter 7: Stop Pretending, Start Living 109
Chapter 8: Busyness Breaks You—Align Your Actions..................123
Chapter 9: Do Less, Achieve More, and Stop Playing Small 141
Chapter 10: The Ripple Effect: Elevate Yourself, Elevate Everyone
    Around You..155

The End of Proving. The Start of Choosing............................167
Appendix: Resources for Support and Healing 175
Acknowledgments 177
PowerShift in Organizations: A Guide for Leaders, Teams, and ERGs ...180
PowerShift Book Club and Discussion Guide: Gather. Reflect. Shift.......182

AUTHOR'S NOTE

The stories in this book are raw for a reason—and they are not just mine, but echoes of what so many women carry in silence. As you read, you may feel old wounds rise to the surface. That's not failure. That's truth asking to be felt.

I know what it's like to push it all down, to believe that asking for help equals weakness. But here's what I learned the hard way: Real strength is knowing you don't have to do it alone. My healing didn't begin until I dismantled that belief and gave myself permission to be supported.

If any part of this book stirs something inside you that feels heavy, please don't ignore it. Reach out to a therapist, healthcare provider, or trauma-informed professional.

You deserve support. You deserve healing. You deserve to feel safe—not just in the world, but within yourself.

This book is about choosing yourself. Sometimes that starts by asking for help.

gia

INTRODUCTION

As women, we're often taught that success is something we earn by proving. Hustle harder. Do it all. Be grateful. Don't forget to smile. And maybe—like me—you did exactly that.

I was suffocating under a life that looked perfect but felt impossible. Maybe you know the feeling: that quiet panic that whispers, *What am I doing? Why does this feel so heavy?* This book is the answer to that whisper.

You might think you're managing it all. But the truth is, most women are settling—not by choice, but by exhaustion. We are stretched too thin, carrying too much, and compensating in silence. We are diluted. Saturated. Our energy pulled in a hundred directions. Our focus fractured. Our purpose buried beneath busyness. But here's what I've realized: When we're spread that thin, we cannot live in alignment. We cannot lead with power. We cannot create the impact we were born for.

I didn't arrive at this realization by chance. I arrived the hard way—through moments that cracked me open, stripped away the illusions, and forced me to question everything I thought I knew about success, worth, and identity.

My wake-up call didn't just shift my life—it rewired my mission. What started as a personal reckoning became the

INTRODUCTION

foundation for my work as a coach, speaker, and researcher. I've now guided hundreds of high-achieving women through this same process, helping them dismantle the conditioning that's been driving their exhaustion. They come to me saying things like, "I don't even know what I want," "I don't know who I am anymore," and "I'm terrified to slow down." Sound familiar? I'll tell you what I tell them: That's not weakness—that's honesty. And that's where the shift starts.

> • • • •
> **That's not weakness— that's honesty. And that's where the shift starts.**
> • • • •

This isn't a book for women who just want to manage burnout or get better at productivity. It's for women who are unknowingly settling—stretched so thin they've mistaken busyness for purpose and exhaustion for achievement. It's for the women who are tired of performing for approval, tired of chasing success by everyone else's definition, and tired of carrying the invisible weight at work and at home. This is for women who are done playing by rules they never agreed to. Done shrinking, diluting, and overfunctioning.

It's for women who feel the pull, the nudge that says *there's more than this.*

This book isn't about balance or managing all the weight. It's about power. It's not meant to change your schedule. It's meant to change how you lead. To change the impact you make. It's about making a shift so complete, so unapologetic, that you never settle again.

Welcome to *PowerShift*.

INTRODUCTION

Every chapter in this book is part of the shift. It's not theory. It's action. It's not another thing on your to-do list; it's the reason you stop writing lists that don't belong to you in the first place.

Shift from proving to choosing.

Shift from busyness to alignment.

Shift from external validation to internal clarity.

Shift from survival mode to thriving.

Shift from chaos to purpose and power.

You've spent your life proving, performing, and carrying weight that was never yours.

If you've been waiting for permission to stop settling, this is it. If you've been waiting for the right moment to shift, this is it.

You are a PowerShifter.

A PowerShifter is the woman who finally says, "Enough."

She doesn't ask for permission. She doesn't apologize for protecting her peace or honoring her priorities. She no longer measures her worth by busyness or sacrifice.

> **A PowerShifter is the woman who finally says, "Enough."**

A PowerShifter
- dismantles the Never-Enough Cycle.
- refuses to carry what isn't hers.
- leads with clarity, alignment, and bold intention.
- drops the guilt, the shoulds, and the pressure.
- amplifies her impact by focusing on what matters— and letting go of the rest.

INTRODUCTION

She knows that proving is a trap and choosing is freedom. She leads with clarity and without apology. She doesn't just chase success, she redefines it.

PowerShifter (noun): A woman who cuts through the noise, challenges the status quo, and redefines success on her own terms. A PowerShifter is part of something bigger than herself. She creates ripple effects that elevate teams, transform cultures, and inspire others to rise. She sets new standards. She doesn't blend in. She shifts the conversation. She chooses alignment over busyness, impact over distraction, and purpose over proving. She leads authentically—and the world follows.

> • • • •
> **Shift doesn't happen when you're ready. It happens when you're done settling.**
> • • • •

Shift doesn't happen when you're ready. It happens when you're done settling. The moment you stop proving and start choosing, the shift begins—and nothing stays the same.

Becoming a PowerShifter isn't about permission. It's about choosing different. And when you do, you show every girl and woman watching that she can too.

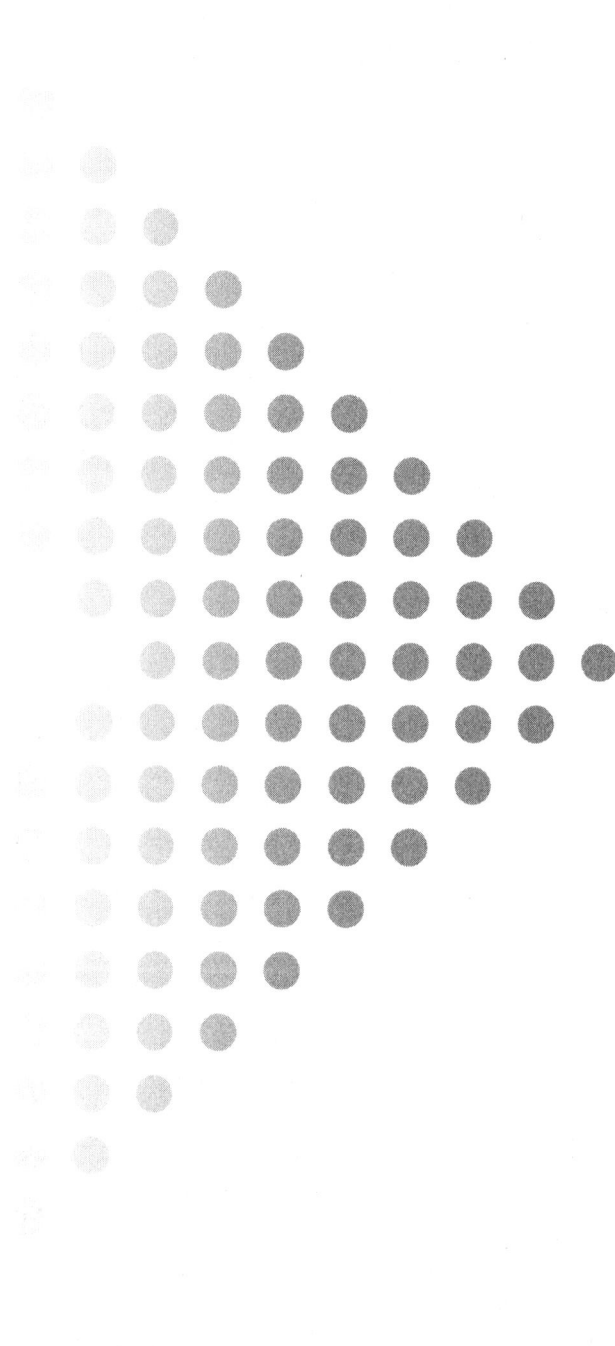

PART I

SHIFT HAPPENS WHEN YOU'RE DONE SETTLING

CHAPTER 1

THE MASKS WE WEAR— AND WHY THEY'RE SUFFOCATING YOU

I didn't burn out because I was weak.

I burned out because I was living an identity I outgrew. Actually, a whole collection of them:

- The baby of the family—easygoing, agreeable, never a problem
- The responsible one—carrying weight that wasn't mine, praised for being "so mature," while suffocating under pressure
- The independent one—the girl who handled everything, who never needed help and wouldn't accept it if it was offered
- The stoic one—holding it all together, even when it hurt
- The good girl—obedient, accommodating, silencing myself to keep others comfortable

- The doer—always in motion, chasing perfection, unable to sit still without guilt whispering that I should be doing more
- The caretaker—tending to everyone else's needs, while ignoring my own

Those identities made me successful. They also made me exhausted, resentful, and disconnected from myself. And here's the truth nobody tells you: Those masks? They start as protection, coping mechanisms we develop when we are young to feel safe, accepted, and worthy. But over time, what once protected us begins to confine us.

Every mask I wore was a survival mechanism. An identity I acquired to feel safe, loved, and worthy. Because somewhere along the way, I learned that just *being* wasn't enough—I had to *do*. To earn.

These were my masks. But I know you have yours too. They may look different, but the weight is the same. It is the pressure to perform, please, and protect—until it buries who you really are. And for many of us, those patterns run deeper than habit. They are echoes of unresolved trauma—unspoken rules etched deep: *Stay small. Be helpful. Keep the peace. Don't need too much.*

Many of us learned that performing was safer than pausing. Pleasing was a shield. Overachieving offered control in an uncertain world. It got us far...but it also kept us stuck.

CHAPTER 1

At some point, those masks stopped serving us and started suffocating us. Maybe you're still wearing a few of them. The question is, Are they still protecting you, or are they holding you back? It's time to find out.

I firmly believe most high-achieving women aren't just ambitious—they're survivors. They grew up learning that love, safety, and approval were earned, not given. They were the "good girls," the responsible ones, the caretakers—not because they wanted to be, but because they *had* to be. They learned early on that being useful kept them safe. So they performed. They pleased. They overfunctioned. And it worked. Until it didn't.

Now they're grown women, CEOs, founders, mothers, leaders—still playing the same survival game they learned as girls. Perhaps that's why you struggle to say no. That's why your calendar is full of things that drain you. That's why you *feel guilty when you stop*. Because some part of you still believes that if you stop doing it all, if you dare to prioritize yourself—you'll be abandoned. Rejected. Not enough. And until you face it head-on, no strategy in the world will save you.

You can color-code your calendar all you want. You can meditate, journal, drink green juice, go to yoga, and create perfect to-do lists. But if the little girl inside you still believes her worth depends on doing and pleasing, you'll sabotage yourself *every time*. There are a lot of books out there about changing your habits. This is not one of them. Instead, it's about reprogramming your operating system.

It's Not About Balance, It's About Power

I had everything on paper: the title, the career, the family. And then one day I hit rock bottom and asked myself, *How the hell did I get here?*

I wasn't just burned out. I was broken. Not by my ambition, but by the lie I had been sold my whole life:

"You just need to do more."

"You can have it all—if you just juggle better."

"Work–life balance is the key to fulfillment."

Let's get one thing straight: *Balance is bullshit.*

Balance is just code for "carry more—and smile while you do it." The definition of balance according to Dictionary.com:

> **Balance (noun):** A state of equilibrium; equal distribution of weight, amount, etc.

• • • •

PowerShifters don't have balance. They have *clarity*.

• • • •

Sounds great in theory. But in real life? This definition of balance is absurd. It suggests that every area of our lives should get equal energy, that we should distribute ourselves perfectly among work, family, personal growth, friendships, self-care, and ambition. As if life were some delicate scale that we could just tweak to achieve harmony.

Balance is a moving target. A myth designed to keep high-achieving women chasing an impossible standard. No matter how much we plan, something always tilts the scale. A sick

CHAPTER 1

child. A demanding boss. A personal crisis. Or maybe just sheer exhaustion from constantly proving our worth.

PowerShifters don't have balance. They have *clarity*. They know what matters most and they focus on it. They stop wasting time on obligations that drain them. They shift from proving to living. And that's exactly what this book is meant to help you do.

This isn't another productivity hack. It's a reckoning. A guide to breaking free from the never-enough cycle so you can stop doing *everything* and start doing *what actually matters*. Because the more capable you are, the more others will ask you to carry. The more you carry, the more praise you'll get. The more praise you get, the more you'll pile on—until you are crushed beneath the weight of your own busyness.

That's not success. That's self-abandonment.

And it doesn't matter how many promotions you get, how many goals you crush, or how many gold stars you collect. If you're still performing for love, approval, or safety, it will never be enough.

The truth is simple but brutal: You've been living a life built on someone else's rules. Rules that told you to keep the peace, be the good girl, work harder, prove yourself, and carry more than anyone should. Rules that rewarded your exhaustion and praised your self-neglect. Rules that were never designed for you to thrive—only to function, produce, and serve.

> • • • •
>
> **You've been living a life built on someone else's rules.**
>
> • • • •

Here's the thing: You cannot fix a construct that was never built for you. Instead, you dismantle it.

You dismantle the expectations that keep you small. You release the obligations you never agreed to carry. You shed the false identities that no longer serve you.

But dismantling takes courage. Because when you start pulling the pieces apart, everything that was hiding underneath will show up.

The fear.

The resentment.

The grief over time lost.

The quiet anger at all the ways you abandoned yourself to meet impossible standards.

That means the work is working.

I'm not here to teach you to balance better. I'm here to help you dismantle what's been suffocating you—and rebuild something that finally fits.

And here's the first step: Stop apologizing for what you no longer want to carry.

You will disappoint people. You will challenge norms. You will make others uncomfortable.

Let them be uncomfortable. Let them question you. Let them adjust.

Because if you don't dismantle the lie now, it will dismantle you later. And I promise you, you are not here to break. You are here to build. Because you don't need balance.

You need alignment.

You need boundaries.

You need truth.

CHAPTER 1

And you need to reclaim the identity you never got to choose, and build it on your terms, not survival instincts.

Spoiler alert: I didn't write this book to make you feel good. I wrote this book to make you feel awake. Because if you're honest, you already know that what you're doing isn't working. You're tired of "balancing." Tired of proving. Tired of playing the game and still feeling empty.

> • • • •
> **Be willing to let go of the woman they told you to be...so you can become the woman you were meant to be.**
> • • • •

I'm going to show you exactly why it's happening, what it's costing you, and how to finally break free. But first, I need you to do one thing: Be willing to let go of the woman they told you to be...so you can become the woman you were meant to be.

My World Shifted

My gaze flitted between the nurse's station and my nearly three-year-old daughter, who had lain limp in the sterile hospital bed for the past four hours, struggling to breathe even with medication. I felt torn, caught between wanting answers and desperately wanting to comfort her. Time stretched into an eternity. The door finally opened. The ER doctor entered with a gentle smile—but not the kind of smile I had been hoping for.

"Mrs. Lacqua," she began, "your daughter is not responding to treatment. I've consulted with the intensivist upstairs, and we need to admit her to the Pediatric ICU."

The rest of her words blurred into the rhythmic beeping of the monitors, a sound that filled the room and seemed to drain all sense of control I once had. Everything went blurry. My world suddenly felt like it was crashing down around me.

We were in the PICU. Machines hummed. Nurses moved quickly. I sat frozen—not just in fear for her, but in shock at myself. I had been holding everything together for so long, convincing myself I could carry it all—the career, the responsibilities, the pressure—and it caught up with me in the most brutal way possible. My daughter couldn't breathe, and I realized, neither could I.

I had built a life on proving, pleasing, and performing. But in that PICU, the truth smacked me across the face: I was suffocating under the weight of success I no longer wanted to carry.

That moment broke me open.

I had always been a high achiever—someone accustomed to managing multiple roles with ease. As a mother, as a businesswoman, and as a problem solver, I was used to juggling responsibilities. I prided myself on being the one who could get things done. I was the fixer. No problem was too big.

But in that moment, sitting beside my daughter, I was powerless. I couldn't fix this. And that thought hit me harder than anything else. I had spent my whole life building a career and a personal life based on doing more, achieving more, and constantly checking things off my list. But here I was, unable to control the one thing that mattered most.

It was 2 a.m. I hadn't eaten or slept in hours. But none of that mattered. Not the emails piling up in my inbox, not

CHAPTER 1

the deadlines I had to meet, not the to-do lists that had once consumed me. All that mattered was her.

As I sat in that cold, quiet room, everything I thought I knew about life and success began to unravel.

I had believed in the idea that I could do it all. But somewhere along the way, that idea had morphed into an expectation. *You have to do it all.* So I did. I hustled. I achieved. I perfected the balancing act. Or so I thought.

> **Seventy-five percent of the women I surveyed admitted to feeling the need to "grin and bear it."**

In that moment, the balancing act didn't feel balanced. I realized I had been chasing a version of success that wasn't mine. I had become so consumed by the pursuit of "more" that I lost sight of what really mattered. I wasn't thriving—I was merely surviving.

It's hard to admit this, but like so many high-achieving women, I didn't slow down. I didn't heed the call. My daughter's recovery should've been my wake-up moment, but instead, I did what I'd been conditioned to do: I pushed forward. I got back to business as usual, back to proving I could hold it all, carry it all, be it all. I rationalized the fear, compartmentalized the trauma, and doubled down on performance. I told myself I was fine—until my body made it clear I wasn't. That's the thing about ignoring alignment: It doesn't go away. It waits.

● ● ●

I know I'm not the only woman who's felt crushed under impossible expectations.

I lived it. You're living it. And 75 percent of the women I surveyed admitted to feeling the need to "grin and bear it." But what if we stopped bearing it? What if we stopped calling it strength and started calling it what it really is—self-abandonment?

> • • • •
> **If you feel lost, you're probably following someone else's map.**
> • • • •

Here's where PowerShifters choose differently. This is where you start choosing differently too.

This resilience, often expected and celebrated, highlights an unsustainable reality. The root? A deeply entrenched prioritization of "doing it all"—at the expense of women's emotional and physical well-being.

But what if I told you there's a way out?

If you feel lost, you're probably following someone else's map. We're not here to keep carrying it all. We're here to carry what matters—and nothing else.

Life Is Always Speaking—Are You Listening?

The signs are everywhere. Sometimes they're loud: burnout, breakdowns, lightning strikes (literally). Sometimes they're subtle: a quiet nudge, a restless feeling, a moment of envy when you see someone else living a life that seems more aligned.

That pull you feel? That whisper that says, *There's more for you than this.* It's not random. It's not silly. It's guidance.

CHAPTER 1

The problem is, most of us are too busy proving, pleasing, and performing to pay attention. We push past the whispers until life throws a brick.

But here's what I've learned: Every challenge, every disruption, every crack in your routine isn't happening *to* you, it's happening *for* you. The tough seasons aren't punishments. They're invitations. Opportunities to pause, reflect, and ask:

What is this trying to teach me?

What part of me is ready to evolve?

What have I been ignoring that's begging to be heard?

Pain, frustration, and even longing show up to reveal the places where you're misaligned or playing small. And if you're brave enough to listen, those moments will lead you toward what's next. So if you feel a pull or a nudge, pay attention. The question isn't, Why is this happening to me? It's, What door is this opening for me?

You can ignore it, resist it, and wait for the breakdown…or you can get curious and start walking through.

Listen to What's Pulling You

Before life throws bricks, it whispers. Take a moment to tune in and listen. Pause, quiet the noise, and hear what's calling you—not from your to-do list, but from your soul. Clarity doesn't come from overthinking. It comes from listening. If you're willing, I invite you to join me in this moment.

The Voice You've Been Drowning Out

Find a quiet place where you won't be interrupted.

Sit comfortably and close your eyes.

Take a deep breath—in through your nose...out through your mouth.

Let your shoulders drop.

Let your jaw soften.

Let the noise of the day fade into the background.

Now, imagine standing in a wide-open field.

It's quiet here.

The air is still.

There's nothing to do.

No one to please.

No expectations.

Ahead of you, you see a small light, flickering but steady.

This light represents the thing that's been tugging at you.

The part of you that knows there's more.

Walk slowly toward it.

With each step, feel the weight on your shoulders getting lighter.

The proving...

The pressure...

The expectations...

All falling away.

As you reach the light, ask yourself gently:

- *What truth have I been carrying that's ready to be spoken?*
- *What gift or impact is trying to come through me?*
- *What would I create or become if I stopped holding back?*

Listen.

Don't force answers—just notice what comes up. A word. A feeling. An image. A color. Trust it.

CHAPTER 1

Place your hand over your heart and say to yourself: *I don't have to have it all figured out. I only have to listen. The rest will follow.*

Take one more deep breath. When you're ready, open your eyes.

Write down whatever came up—trust it, even if it doesn't make sense yet. You don't need to have all the answers right now. You only need to listen.

PowerShifters don't force clarity; they make space for it. They don't ignore the whispers. They get curious, listen. They stop long enough to hear the whisper...and then they move.

The next step is yours. Shift happens the moment you stop resisting what's trying to come through you.

Shift happens when you follow the pull instead of fighting it.

• • • •

PowerShifters don't ignore the whispers. They get curious, listen, and move.

• • • •

CHAPTER 2

∙∙∙∙∙∙∙∙∙∙∙∙

SHE'S RUNNING THE SHOW— BUT SHE'S NOT YOU

You've been following her lead for years.

The good girl.

The overachiever.

The caretaker.

The woman who never drops the ball, never asks for help, and never lets anyone down.

She got you here. She made you successful. But here's the hard truth: She's not you.

She's your survival self—built from old stories, unspoken rules, and coping.

We don't wear masks because we want to; we wear them because, at some point, we had to. For many women, that "had to" runs deeper than pressure to achieve or please. It's about safety. In my national research study, almost *half* of women reported experiencing sexual assault, harassment, or unwanted advances. *Almost half.* Which means if it didn't happen to you, it happened to a woman sitting next to you.

And here's what those experiences teach us, without ever saying a word: *Be nice. Don't make waves. Don't draw attention. Smile to make others more comfortable. Stay small. Stay agreeable. Stay safe.*

But it doesn't stop there.

We learn to keep people at arm's length. *Don't let them in. Don't show them the real you.*

We learn to be suspicious of kindness. *Be wary of new people. Trust no one until they prove otherwise.*

We learn to scan the room before we speak. *Always look over your shoulder. Know where the exits are. Walk fast, keys and phone in hand.*

We don't adopt these masks and patterns by accident. They're learned behaviors—scripts we write early in life to protect ourselves. I call them *survival scripts*.

They tell us who to be, how to act, and what parts of ourselves to hide, all in the name of staying safe, accepted, and in control. At first, these scripts serve us. They help us navigate uncertainty, avoid danger, and hold things together when we feel powerless.

But what once protected us eventually confines us. And unless we stop and question those scripts, we end up living by rules that were written in moments of fear, not moments of truth.

••••

In my national research study, almost *half* of women reported experiencing sexual assault, harassment, or unwanted advances.

••••

CHAPTER 2

For many women, those scripts are shaped not just by expectations, but by experiences no one ever talks about.

You are not what happened to you. You are who you decide to become beyond it.

PowerShifters name those scripts for what they are: fear-based rules written in moments when choice was taken away. And then...they choose differently.

You can't shift your life until you unmask who's really running the show. So let's meet her. And then let's decide if she's coming with you...or staying behind.

"I'm Fine. It's Fine. Everything's Fine."

How many times have you said "I'm fine" when you were anything but? We say it on autopilot. Because admitting we're not OK feels like weakness. Because we're scared someone might actually stop and ask us to feel it. Because we've been conditioned to keep going, keep smiling, keep holding it all together.

"I'm fine" is often the loudest cry for help in disguise.

There was a point in my corporate career when the constant business travel was simply part of the job—until it became part of the problem. Back-to-back trips, red-eye flights, hotel points, living out of a suitcase—I wore it like a badge of honor. But underneath that hustle was a weight I didn't understand yet.

My girls were little, and every trip felt heavier than the last. But I kept going, convinced this was what success looked like. Until one morning, I found myself in the back of a black Lincoln Town Car, quietly pulling away from my house at

5 a.m. The house was silent. It was dark. Everyone still asleep. And for some reason, that darkness and silence broke me.

It started with a few quiet tears. Then a sniffle. Then full-on ugly crying. The kind where you can't breathe, and you're trying to be quiet but failing miserably. What I didn't realize at the time was that this wasn't just exhaustion. It was the weight of my own unresolved childhood wounds eating away at me. Every time I left home, I was retraumatizing myself in ways I couldn't yet name.

The driver glanced at me in the rearview mirror, equal parts concerned and terrified, and softly asked, "Ma'am...are you OK?"

Without missing a beat, through ugly sobs, shreds of tissues, and mascara streaks, I blurted out, "Yeah, I'm fine."

There was a pause so long you could feel him questioning all his life choices. Then he nodded slowly and said, "I can stop for coffee."

Honestly, bless that man. He understood the assignment.

Have you had a moment like that? When, out of nowhere, you just felt overwhelmed, where you broke down but kept pressing forward, telling everyone including yourself, "I'm fine"? PowerShifters learn to replace "I'm fine" with honesty—with themselves first.

Ask yourself:
- *Why am I still saying "I'm fine" when I'm exhausted, overwhelmed, or running on fumes?*
- *What would happen if I told the truth instead?*

Because shift happens the moment you stop pretending.

CHAPTER 2

Complete this sentence without censoring yourself:
I am the woman who...

What words come up? Do they reflect who you are or who you think you're *supposed* to be?

If you come up blank, pause and know this: You're not alone—that silence is the residue of years spent adapting, accommodating, and performing. It's what happens when you've been so focused on being who the world needs you to be that you lose sight of who you actually are.

• • • •

PowerShifters learn to replace "I'm fine" with honesty—with themselves first.

• • • •

What you believe about yourself shapes every decision in your life, your leadership, and your organization.

This is where PowerShifters begin—not with perfection, but with honesty. Start there.

The Stories That Built You

Early on in life, I came to believe that my place in the world wasn't guaranteed—I had to earn it.

I was raised by my aunt and uncle, a dynamic that shaped my sense of self in ways I couldn't fully comprehend at the time. They were loving and supportive and did everything in their power to provide for me, and for that I am eternally grateful.

Being taken in as a child by family members should have made me feel chosen, loved, secure. Instead, it wired me for feelings of unworthiness. I carried the quiet but unshakable belief that I had to prove my value, that my presence was a privilege I had to justify. Every achievement, every sacrifice, every impossible standard I met wasn't about success—it was about survival.

Years later, I came to realize that the circumstances surrounding my upbringing instilled in me a set of beliefs and narratives that would persist for decades. These stories weren't overtly imposed on me but rather quietly woven into the fabric of my identity, influencing my actions and decisions in subtle yet profound ways.

One of the heaviest stories I carried was the quiet belief that I wasn't enough—not as I was, not without proving something extraordinary.

As a child, I knew I was different from my peers. I wasn't raised by my biological parents, and that fact followed me like a shadow. When people asked innocent questions about my family—"Why do you live with them?" and "Where are your parents?"—I didn't just stumble over my answers. I didn't *have* answers.

In today's world, blended families and nontraditional upbringings are common conversations, but back when feathered bangs, Walkmans, and *MacGyver* ruled my world, it was unusual, awkward, and loaded with questions I couldn't answer. I was desperate to appear "normal." So I learned to smile, to smooth over the awkwardness, to be the agreeable, responsible, high-achieving girl who made everyone else comfortable.

Underneath that performance was a deep fracture—a constant, gnawing feeling that I was the outsider in my

CHAPTER 2

own life. I told myself that if I could just excel, if I could be exceptional, maybe I'd earn the belonging I never felt. So I chased that version of "enough" relentlessly. I sacrificed rest, ignored my needs, pushed past every limit, and wore my busyness and perfectionism like armor.

That chase was never about ambition. It was about filling a hole created from the belief that I was incomplete, flawed, or unworthy.

I learned that you can't outrun the parts of your story you don't understand. And the longer you try, the heavier they become.

As children, when something feels off or unsafe, we don't blame the world. We blame ourselves. We create stories to make sense of the pain, stories that say, "It's my fault." But those were survival narratives, not truths.

These stories didn't just shape my internal world; they bled into the way I engaged with the world externally too. They influenced how I showed up in relationships, at work, and in my daily life. I believed I had to do more, achieve more, be more, and in that relentless pursuit, I lost sight of who I truly was beneath all the layers of *shoulds* and *musts*.

Even in college, the pattern was already set. They called me "Mother Hen." I was the one making sure everyone got home safe, holding hair back in bathroom stalls, double-checking that the door was locked, and being the responsible one—while everyone else let loose.

The truth, though, was that the stories I carried with me were just that—stories. They weren't reality. But they were *my* reality for a long time, coloring the lens through which I viewed myself and the world around me.

It wasn't until later—after years of burnout and an awakening through a personal crisis—that I began to realize how deeply these stories had shaped me. And it was through this awareness that I started to rewrite my narrative, reimagining who I was *beyond* the stories I had been telling myself.

The work of reinvention wasn't easy. It meant confronting uncomfortable truths, unearthing the limiting beliefs I'd held about myself for so long, and allowing space for a new identity to emerge. But through this process, I came to understand that our stories don't define us unless we let them. The power lies in our ability to shift our narratives, to see ourselves from a place of wholeness rather than deficiency, and to step into the truth of who we were always meant to be.

This theme of *stories*—the ones we carry with us and those we choose to rewrite—became a through-line in my journey. It's not just my story that matters; it's how we all confront, challenge, and ultimately transform the stories we've carried with us. In doing so, we can create new narratives, ones that empower, liberate, and guide us toward the truest versions of ourselves.

For most of my life, I was searching, clawing for answers outside of myself. I believed clarity, validation, and belonging lived somewhere *out there*...in other people's approval, in achievement, in being needed, in being perfect.

At twenty-two, I met my biological father for the first time. I naively thought that moment would complete the puzzle for me, that sitting across from him at a café in New York City

CHAPTER 2

would unlock some hidden truth about who I was. But afterward, I felt hollow. I realized, with a quiet ache in my chest: *I still have no idea who I am.*

I had spent years building an identity out of other people's expectations, becoming who I thought I needed to be to earn love, respect, and safety. But standing in front of the man whose absence had defined much of my story, I felt the weight of every story I didn't write for myself. I had been shaped by circumstances I didn't choose. I had been performing roles I never questioned.

Sadly, I'm not alone in that. So many of us spend our lives looking for someone or something to hand us the answer—the missing piece that will make us feel whole.

I thought meeting my biological dad would heal the hole inside me. But no single moment, no reunion, no external revelation can do that. Because wholeness doesn't come from outside. It comes from trusting yourself enough to stop asking others who you are.

I had been conditioned, like so many women, to ignore that voice. I was taught that being "good" meant being agreeable. That questioning made me difficult. That my feelings were "too much." Over time, I learned to doubt my instincts, silence my intuition, and defer to others. I didn't just lose trust in myself; I never knew how to build it in the first place.

And that was the real loss. Not missing answers from someone else, but missing the answers that had been inside me all along, buried beneath years of performance and permission-seeking.

But it wasn't just conditioning. It was hardship. It was trauma. When you grow up adapting to survive, you learn to look outward instead of inward. You learn that your instincts don't matter as much as what will keep you safe, accepted, or loved. You become hyper-aware of others while becoming a stranger to yourself. The more I experienced, the more I silenced my own needs, my own feelings, my own intuition—because sometimes survival requires shutting yourself down.

So I stopped listening. I silenced my instincts in favor of logic, proof, and external validation. I ignored the gut feelings that told me when something was wrong, when I needed rest, when I was out of alignment. I became an expert at looking outward for direction—chasing achievement, perfection, and approval—while feeling increasingly disconnected from myself. And by the time I needed my inner voice the most, I could no longer hear her. She was buried under the never-ending to-do lists.

> **I was paying a debt I was never supposed to owe.**

Rebuilding that trust with myself wasn't easy. It required unlearning years of conditioning that told me I had to prove my worth, seek permission, and make choices based on what would make others comfortable. It meant confronting the survival mechanisms that once kept me safe but no longer served me. It meant getting quiet enough to listen to the voice I had buried beneath expectation, fear, and doubt. And when

CHAPTER 2

I finally heard her again, I realized she had never left. She had been waiting for me to remember that I already had everything I needed within me. I wasn't just striving; I was paying a debt I was never supposed to owe.

That belief followed me into every space I entered. In my career, I climbed the corporate ladder, not just to succeed, but to *deserve* my seat at the table. When I made vice president at thirty-six—while pregnant—I should have celebrated. Instead, I doubled down, terrified that if I slowed down, I'd lose my place. If I wasn't constantly proving, would I still be valuable?

> **Part of becoming a PowerShifter is releasing those old stories and realizing *it was never your fault.***

I was still trying to earn my keep. And that's when I saw it for what it was: a lie.

Part of becoming a PowerShifter is releasing those old stories and realizing *it was never your fault.*

We all carry stories we didn't write. Stories we inherited from family, society, circumstance. Stories we've told ourselves. Some are loud. And some are so quiet, they feel like truth.

EXAMINE YOUR STORIES

Ask yourself:
- What story did I inherit about who I am? Who I am not?
- Where did it come from?
- What has that story cost me?
- Am I ready to question it...and choose something different?

You don't have to keep carrying a story that was never yours to begin with.

CHAPTER 3

THE COST OF CARRYING IT ALL

Our culture values busyness. We wear our overscheduled calendars like badges of honor. But when everything is a priority, nothing is a priority.

Writing this book was like confronting the woman I once was—someone who thought success meant never saying no, ever. As I reflect on my journey, I realize that the story I'm telling you now is one I couldn't have written until I went through the unraveling. The unraveling that started the day I got lost—physically and metaphorically.

That's when I stopped trying to manage my time and started managing my energy. I learned to prioritize what mattered most—my family, my health, my career, and caring for myself. I healed. I cut out the unnecessary, the energy-draining commitments. I aligned my life to my purpose. I shifted my perspective.

I realized that my kids would rather have a fun mom than a spotless house. I stopped thinking that "downtime" was lazy or that asking for help was a weakness. I started to define my life by how I wanted to feel, not by how much I could accomplish.

This wasn't just about getting my health back on track—it was about reclaiming my life, about being present, about being authentic. It was about transformation. For me, this reflection was a wake-up call. It was a reminder that my health, my peace of mind, and my relationships are far more important than the endless to-do lists. And in that realization, I found my way back to myself.

It's time to let the rain fall, to let the challenges shape us into something new. And in doing so, we can grow into the life we were always meant to live. We are more than our responsibilities. We are not defined by what we do, but by who we are. It's time to reflect on what stories we've been telling ourselves and start writing a new narrative—one that's in alignment with our true selves.

> **I could no longer keep running the race that had no finish line.**

Success wasn't working anymore—not if it meant I had to sacrifice my well-being, my sanity, and my relationship with my own soul.

I could no longer keep running the race that had no finish line.

I began to understand that it was time to redefine success—success on my terms. It was time to break free and give myself permission to choose what truly mattered: my health, my happiness, my family, my soul's deep needs. It wasn't going to be easy, but I had no choice. I had to rebuild my life, piece by piece—starting with myself.

CHAPTER 3

This Is Where Shift Begins

Through my personal journey and from the voices of the many high-achieving women I've worked with as a coach, I've come to realize that most of us live in a state of chronic stress and exhaustion. We're driven by ambition, pulled in every direction by external expectations and pressures. We sacrifice so much in the name of success, only to find that we are burned out, unfulfilled, and disconnected from our own needs and bodies. In the process, we lose sight of the true source of fulfillment: our internal compass.

Pain that isn't processed doesn't just sit quietly—it leaks. Like water seeping through the cracks of a foundation, it finds its way into the spaces we don't expect. It shows up in the relentless drive to prove ourselves, in the inability to rest without guilt, in the way we pour into others while leaving ourselves empty. No matter how hard we try to patch the surface with success, busyness, or perfection, the pressure builds until the cracks widen. And eventually, if we don't address the source, the foundation gives way.

For years, I believed that if I just kept moving—kept achieving, kept handling it all—the pain I carried would dissipate. But pain that isn't acknowledged doesn't disappear; it embeds itself in the stories we tell ourselves about who we are and what we deserve. It wasn't until I faced my own fractures that I realized something profound: The cracks weren't just places of weakness—they were spaces for light to enter, for something new to grow.

This is the essence of post-traumatic growth—the idea that from deep struggle, transformation is possible. That pain, when processed and integrated, can become a catalyst for profound change, resilience, and purpose. Trauma can shape us, but it doesn't have to define us. In fact, the very experiences that tried to break us can become the foundation for something even stronger.

True healing didn't come from proving I was stronger than my pain. It came from allowing myself to feel it, understand it, and ultimately, transform it. The moment I stopped asking, *Why did this happen to me?* and started asking, *How can I use this to help others? How can I use what I've been through to create something meaningful? How can I take what once held me back and turn it into my driving force? What change can I create because of what I've been through?* everything shifted. My pain became my purpose—not because I needed suffering to justify my worth, but because I chose to alchemize it into something meaningful.

> **My own fractures... weren't just places of weakness—they were spaces for light to enter, for something new to grow.**

I decided to leave my corporate job, but I didn't just walk away from a job. I walked away from a corporate career I had spent nearly two decades building—one title, one late night, one business trip, one stressful meeting at a time.

I earned every promotion, every seat at the table, every ounce of respect—often in rooms where I was the only woman, and usually the youngest. I built a reputation as the one who could handle anything. And I did. I led teams, managed crises, launched new initiatives, delivered results. I made vice president while pregnant with my second daughter. I rose not because it was easy, but because I never let it not be.

I had done everything "right." But still, something inside was gnawing at me.

So I didn't leave because I couldn't handle it. I left because I finally realized I wasn't meant to just *handle* it. I was meant to change it.

I left because I knew deep down that there was more for me—not more to do, but more to *become*.

For many high-achieving women, work isn't just a paycheck, it's proof.

Proof that the sacrifices were worth it.

Proof that they belong.

Proof that they've "made it."

And that's exactly what makes it so hard to walk away, even when the job is slowly eroding your health, your joy, and your sense of self.

We don't just invest time in our careers, we invest identity. Years of education. Sleepless nights. Weeks away from our babies. It's not just a role. It's a piece of who we are. For some, it's *all* of who we are. And letting it go? That can feel like failure.

So we stay. Even when we're burned out.

Even when we're operating in cultures that reward overfunctioning and ignore well-being.

Even when our bodies are screaming what our calendars won't admit: This is no longer sustainable.

Because we've been taught that leaving means giving up. That rest means weakness. That our value is tied to our output. And underneath all of that? Fear.

Fear of losing financial security.

Fear of disappointing everyone who expected us to keep climbing.

Fear that without the title, we'll lose the proof that we're enough.

But here's the truth: *Staying is powerful when it's aligned.* When it's intentional. When it's part of your mission.

For some women, shaking the old model from inside the boardroom is exactly where they're meant to be. That brings a smile to my face because we *need* women in those rooms, raising standards, disrupting norms, and modeling new ways to lead.

But for me? The pull was different.

I could've stayed. I could've continued climbing, earning, delivering—and I know I would have driven impact from the inside. (If you haven't already noticed, I'm a disruptor by nature.)

But this wasn't about power. It was about truth.

This wasn't about leaving as the only answer. It was about *listening*—and being honest enough to follow what I heard.

Of course, if you'd told me then that I'd become a children's book author, I would've laughed out loud. But that's the power of alignment: It introduces you to parts of yourself you've never met.

This is the work. Not just surviving what broke us, but reclaiming ourselves in the process. Not just moving forward, but moving forward with intention—rewriting the narratives shaped in pain and replacing them with ones built on power, healing, and alignment. Turning pain into purpose isn't about erasing what hurt us; it's about using it as fuel to build something greater, something that no longer keeps us trapped in the past but propels us into the future we deserve.

Superwoman Is Not Real
When you ignore the first call, the second one comes harder. And that second call? It doesn't whisper.

A year after the PICU, I found myself in a very different kind of emergency—one where the crisis wasn't external. It was inside me.

I had pushed through, like I always did. I told myself I was fine, like we all do. I wore the mask, performed the role, kept the plates spinning. But behind the scenes, my body was sending signals I couldn't ignore: heart palpitations, exhaustion, the slow unraveling of someone who had spent too long outrunning herself.

I thought I was invincible. Strong, smart, capable, independent—I could do it all while wearing four-inch heels and running on nothing but five hours of sleep and six cups of coffee. I was on top of my game. I didn't take notes in meetings because I didn't need to. My mind was sharp enough to recall every detail. My purse, keys, and car were always exactly where I left them—neat, organized, and in control. Lists? Those were for people who couldn't manage their lives. Not me. I had it all figured out.

I was the go-to person. The one who never said no—to work, to friends, to family, to anyone who needed my time, expertise, or shoulder. I lived by the motto "I've got this." And by "this," I didn't mean just my own problems. I meant your problems too. Everyone's problems. I was managing it all, effortlessly.

Until one day, I wasn't.

It started with small things. A forgotten password to my computer—a computer I logged on to every morning. Then, I got lost driving my kids to school. It was one of those embarrassing moments, the kind where you know how to get there in your sleep, but somehow, you don't. Next, I accidentally took my once-per-day medication twice in one day. I cut my finger multiple times instead of the vegetables I was cooking for dinner and ended up with stitches. My body was clearly telling me something I wasn't listening to. But I kept going. I woke up with headaches, went to bed with headaches, couldn't sleep, and fell into the same pattern of exhaustion.

Then came the real wake-up call. I boarded my monthly cross-country flight, and ten minutes into the air, I started experiencing heart palpitations. Not the occasional flutter—no, these were constant, unrelenting extra beats. I chalked it up to one of the four medications I was taking for my sinus infection. But the next morning, I still felt it. The palpitations didn't stop.

I came home from that business trip still wired, still running on fumes, and now worried. I dropped my bags, kicked off my heels, and before I could even think about catching my breath, I was already asking myself, *What am I going to make for dinner?*

CHAPTER 3

And then, it hit.

The racing heart.

The shortness of breath.

The cold sweat.

The panic set in. I sank to the floor, heart pounding so loudly I could barely think.

And yet I said nothing. I did *nothing*. I was paralyzed with fear. I was too afraid to admit out loud what I was thinking: *Am I having a heart attack?*

Instead, I lay there on the cold floor, alone with the weight of my own choices. I had spent years sprinting toward success, climbing the ladder, achieving, proving, performing. But in that moment, I wasn't powerful. I was scared. Scared that I had built a life so busy, so demanding, that it was about to take me out. And I don't need to tell you that "scared" is *not* a familiar or comfortable feeling for us high-achieving women.

That moment forced me to face the truth. My Superwoman cape was actually a straitjacket. Spoiler alert: Superwoman isn't real. And she's definitely not me.

What I was carrying wasn't sustainable. And no one was going to lighten the load for me. I had to choose differently or I wouldn't get up off that floor next time.

I sat in the doctor's office, listing symptoms like I was reading off a grocery list: heart racing, can't sleep, always anxious. And then she asked, "How long has this been going on?" I opened my mouth to answer...but nothing came out. Just tears.

Years of buried emotion—the pressure to perform, to be strong, to carry everyone's needs but my own—finally cracked open in that sterile white room. I put my hands over my chest, trying to hold it together, but I couldn't. I wasn't just overwhelmed. I was drowning.

All the times I told myself "I'm fine." All the times I swallowed disappointment, anger, grief. All the masks I had worn—the good girl (she's retired now), the do-er, the one who holds it all together—came crashing down in that moment.

Two weeks passed. I went through it all: the heart monitor, the stress test, two cardiologists, two echocardiograms. Appointment after appointment, searching for something to fix.

And then the call came. My heart was perfectly healthy. What I had been feeling wasn't a heart problem at all. What a relief! But, wait...

It was burnout. The physical manifestation of years of carrying too much, running too hard, and ignoring every whisper from my body that begged me to slow down. Stress, fatigue, self-neglect—all dressed up as ambition and responsibility.

I had been running on empty for too long, convincing myself I could be everything to everyone: The high performer. The dependable one. The one who never breaks.

But I hit a wall—hard.

And here's what hit me even harder: I realized I wasn't there for a diagnosis. I was there because my body was shouting what I refused to say out loud: You can't suppress, avoid, or outwork the truth. It will find you—and it won't whisper.

That day, I didn't just walk away with a prescription. I got a mirror. And I couldn't look away.

CHAPTER 3

I had been so laser-focused on holding everyone else together that I never noticed how far I had abandoned myself. I thought I was invincible. But my body had other plans. That health scare forced me to stop. To question. To finally ask myself:

What am I doing to my body?
What am I doing to my mind?
What am I doing to my life?

And the answer was clear: I was breaking myself trying to hold up everyone and everything else.

I remember it like it was yesterday. I was on the phone with the benefits provider, explaining why I needed to take a leave from work. My voice was shaking as I told her about the panic, the exhaustion, the palpitations. I braced for judgment or surprise.

Instead, she responded flatly, "Oh yeah, I hear that a lot."

I had to pick my jaw up off the floor. What had become my breaking point was just another Monday for her—I was simply one of countless women cracking under the same impossible pressure. That moment landed hard. It wasn't just me. This was systemic.

That phone call became a catalyst, the moment I stopped asking *What's wrong with me?* and started asking *What's wrong with the way we're living?*

Maybe you haven't ended up on a doctor's table. Maybe you haven't felt your heart race out of control or collapsed in tears you can't explain. But I'll bet you've felt the weight. The pressure to carry it all. The exhaustion that creeps in, telling you this is just how life is. You don't need a health scare to wake up.

You just need to stop long enough to ask yourself the question I had been too afraid to face: *What am I doing to myself?*

> ## KEY CONCEPT: COGNITIVE DISSONANCE
>
> The mental discomfort that arises when your actions don't align with your values or beliefs is called cognitive dissonance (as described in *Medical News Today,* https://www.medicalnewstoday.com/articles/326738). Women often experience this when they chase external success while feeling unfulfilled internally. Most women push through, ignoring the warning signs. PowerShifters listen…and choose differently.
>
> **Exercise**
> Write down three areas of your life where you feel tension between what you do and what you truly desire. What story are you telling yourself that keeps you stuck there?

The Price You're Paying

Take a moment to consider the price you've been paying without even realizing it—the energy leaks, the identity fractures, the quiet betrayals. As you think about this, I'm going to help you make a choice: Keep carrying it all until you break…or start shedding what was never yours to hold in the first place.

Let's dig into what this load is really costing you—and why you've been willing to carry it for so long.

CHAPTER 3

Erosion of Self
You've spent so long being who others needed you to be, you've forgotten who you actually are. You make decisions out of obligation, not desire. You say yes automatically and then resent yourself for it. You can't remember the last time you did something without measuring its utility.

Chronic Emotional Suppression
You stuff it down. You power through. But it leaks out—as irritability, anxiety, and moments where you feel like screaming or crying for no reason. You hold space for everyone else's emotions, but never your own. You apologize when you cry. You tell yourself "I'm fine" so often it's practically a mantra.

Hyper-Independence
You don't ask for help because you don't trust anyone will show up. You secretly resent everyone for not helping, while rejecting their help when it's offered. You pride yourself on being self-sufficient, but it's isolating. You've built walls so high, no one can get in—and now you don't know how to take them down.

Achievement Addiction
You chase goals like hits of dopamine—but the high never lasts. You hit the milestone, then immediately move the goalpost. The "next big thing" keeps you distracted from the emptiness. You can't sit still without feeling lazy, behind, or guilty.

Physical Burnout
The palpitations, the insomnia, the headaches? That's your body screaming for what your mind won't give it. Fatigue that sleep doesn't fix. Anxiety you can't rationalize away. Constant tension in your jaw, neck, and shoulders.

Resentment Toward the People You Love
You show up for everyone. Though, at first, you want to be needed—you *need* to be needed—after a while, you start resenting others for needing you so much. You get frustrated with your kids, partner, colleagues. Then you feel guilty for resenting them—which you suppress, and which builds. You end up feeling trapped by the life you built.

Settling (While Telling Yourself You're Winning)
You have the title. The home. The family. The career. But deep down, you know you've settled for exhaustion in place of joy. You tell yourself, *This is just how it is.* You rationalize your misery as the price of success. You're afraid to slow down because then you'd have to face how misaligned it really is.

Lost Intimacy with Yourself and Others
You're never fully present. You're half in, half out, all the time. Conversations feel transactional. You can't remember the last time you sat with yourself without reaching for a phone, laptop, or to-do list. You miss moments because your mind is already on the next task.

CHAPTER 3

Playing Small in Disguise
Overachieving is often just fear of stillness. Constant busyness keeps you from asking, *Am I even living the life I want?* You're too busy to make bold moves. You settle into patterns because disrupting them feels terrifying.

Passing on the Cycle to the Next Generation
Your daughters, your team, the women who watch you—they think this is how it has to be. You're modeling exhaustion as normal. You're teaching others that success equals self-abandonment. The cycle continues...unless you stop it.

• • •

And here's the worst part: No one's going to tell you to stop. Because your overfunctioning serves everyone else. Until you choose differently, the cost is *you*.

Others will never ask you to stop. They will never lighten your load. Because what you do that creates your exhaustion makes their lives easier. Your overgiving keeps everyone else comfortable. Your constant proving props up constructs that were never designed with you in mind. And if you don't stop, if you don't interrupt this pattern, the cost will keep stacking.

Your health.
Your joy.
Your relationships.
Your legacy.

You already know this. You can feel it. You've been carrying the weight so long, you've convinced yourself it's just part of who you are.

It's not. It's part of who you were trained to be. And that's why it's so hard to let go.

If you're tired of carrying weight that was never yours, this is where we shift—together. This is where you give yourself permission to stop.

The courage to break the cycle. Unlearn the rules that never served you. Deconstruct the expectations that suffocate you. Release the masks that no longer fit.

In the next few chapters, I'm going to show you exactly how to do that.

But fair warning: It's going to get uncomfortable. Because the moment you stop carrying what was never yours, you'll finally realize how heavy it really was. And once you feel that weight lift, you'll never settle for it again.

CHAPTER 4

THE NEVER-ENOUGH CYCLE— HOW YOU GOT HERE AND WHY IT'S BREAKING YOU

You do it all. You say yes, pick up the slack, and keep pushing even when you're running on fumes. And yet it never feels like enough, does it? If you've ever found yourself crossing off tasks but still feeling behind, if praise fuels you but silence terrifies you, if rest feels indulgent and success feels fleeting, you're in it. The Never-Enough Cycle isn't your fault. It's not about what you're doing. It's about what you've been conditioned to believe.

I lived this cycle. But it isn't just *my* pattern—it's yours too. More importantly, it's a cycle that's yours to break.

The Never-Enough Cycle is something that many women, especially high achievers, fall into. It's driven by external pressures and societal expectations. But the worst part is that we internalize this belief—we think that no matter how much we do or achieve, it's never quite enough. This constant cycle of doing more and more without ever feeling fulfilled leads to burnout and chronic overwhelm. We disconnect from our own needs and desires.

Overdoing, overgiving, overproving—the Never-Enough Cycle doesn't end when you achieve more. It ends when you decide you have nothing left to prove.

The day I found myself wearing a heart monitor to work at the age of thirty-eight was the day I was forced to confront a truth I had spent my entire career outrunning: No matter how much I achieved, it never felt like enough. I had been conditioned to measure my worth by my output, my success by my ability to juggle it all without breaking. And yet I found myself breaking.

> • • • •
> **Sixty-nine percent of women reported that no matter their achievements, it feels like it's never enough.**
> • • • •

I share this not because my story is unique, but because it's *not*. Maybe you've found yourself in that same silence, wondering when it became your job to carry it all. The truth? You're not broken. You're operating on old scripts that aren't yours. And now is your chance to release them.

In my national research study, 69 percent of women reported that no matter their achievements, it feels like it's never enough. These working women felt trapped by a narrative that tells us it is never enough, leading us to burnout and exhaustion. And the truth is, most of us don't even realize we're caught in this cycle. We're told to be perfect mothers and high-powered leaders, stay healthy and fit, volunteer, and look good while doing it all.

This isn't just a personal crisis—it's an organizational one. Overloaded women don't just burn out; they leave toxic workplace cultures that drain them. That's turnover, lost talent, and stalled progress.

This relentless chase—always striving, always pushing, never arriving—creates immense stress and cognitive dissonance, forcing us to exist in a perpetual state of proving rather than being. We tell ourselves that if we could just do more, be more, then maybe—just maybe—we'd finally feel worthy. But that finish line keeps moving. The metric for "enough" is a mirage, always shifting further away the closer we get.

KEY CONCEPT: THE NEVER-ENOUGH CYCLE

The Never-Enough Cycle is a psychological and emotional state where an individual consistently feels that their efforts, achievements, and contributions are insufficient, regardless of their accomplishments. This pervasive sense of inadequacy leads to a continuous drive for perfection and higher performance, often at the expense of personal well-being and satisfaction.

Exercise

How do you know if you're stuck in the Never-Enough Cycle? Put a check next to any of the patterns below that sound like you:

- [ ] You check off every goal on your list yet still feel like you're falling behind.
- [ ] You struggle to celebrate your wins because you're already focused on the next thing.
- [ ] Rest feels uncomfortable—like a luxury you haven't earned.
- [ ] You feel guilty for prioritizing yourself, even when you're running on empty.
- [ ] You crave a sense of fulfillment, but you're not sure what that even looks like anymore.

The Origins of the Never-Enough Cycle

The Never-Enough Cycle doesn't come out of nowhere. It's not personality, it's programming. It's conditioning. It's survival. Here's where it begins:

Childhood Conditioning: The First Lessons in Self-Abandonment

Conditioning doesn't begin in the boardroom. It begins in the living room, the classroom, the dining room. It's shaped by parents, teachers, coaches, and culture. And while it's often rooted in love, that doesn't make it any less powerful—or any less damaging.

Even well-meaning adults teach us early on that worth is something we earn, not something we are. That being a "good girl" means being agreeable, helpful, selfless. Low-maintenance and high-performing. That love, praise, and

CHAPTER 4

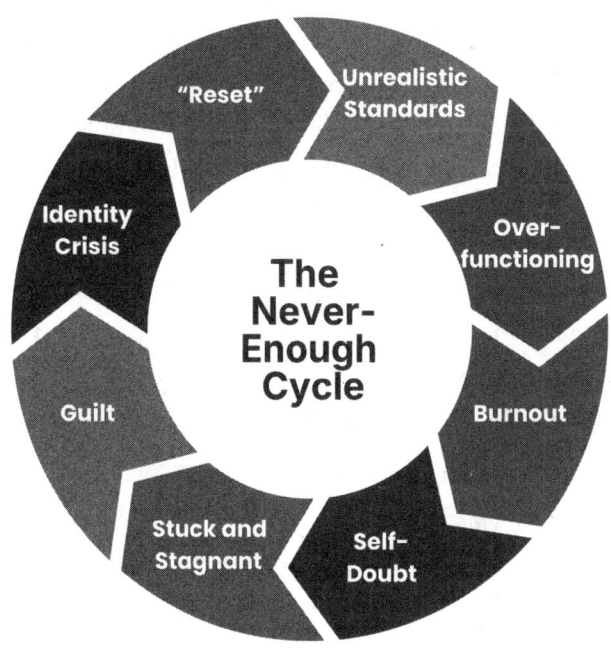

Unrealistic Standards: Setting exceptionally high standards and feeling immense pressure to meet them

Overfunctioning: Taking on too much and neglecting self-care, leading to being overwhelmed

Burnout: Exhausted, depleted, running on empty

Self-Doubt: Questioning your worth, feeling like you're falling behind

Stuck and Stagnant: Lost, unsure what you actually want, paralyzed by indecision

Guilt: Rest feels selfish; slowing down feels wrong

Identity Crisis: If you're not the one who does it all, then who are you?

"Reset": A quick fix (vacation, self-care) to keep going—but nothing changes

belonging are handed out in direct proportion to how easy we are to manage and how well we perform in school and sports.

Many of us were raised by women who carried the weight of entire households, families, and expectations—without complaint. Mothers who did everything. Grandmothers who sacrificed in silence. Single parents who had no choice but to keep going. They didn't always have the language for burnout or boundaries. They had resilience. They had grit. They had survival.

And we watched.

And we learned.

We inherited not just their strength but their stories.

Stories about what it means to be a woman.

> • • • •
> **Even well-meaning adults teach us early on that worth is something we earn, not something we are.**
> • • • •

Stories about what's expected of us.

Stories about what must be sacrificed to be seen as valuable.

Stories about what must be silenced to keep the peace.

This is where the performance began—not out of ego, but out of love, fear, and conditioning. Not to impress, but to belong. This showed itself in several ways:

- *Perfectionism:* You were raised to believe mistakes aren't allowed. You learned to connect your worth to flawless performance.
- *Conditional Love:* You were praised only when you excelled. You learned love is earned, not given.

CHAPTER 4

- *Emotional Neglect:* Often, your needs were not met. You grew up overcompensating—doing, fixing, and achieving to fill an invisible void.

Societal Conditioning: The Impossible Standard
While the roots of overachievement are planted in childhood, society waters them daily with expectations disguised as empowerment.

We were raised on a steady loop of slogans:
- "Girls can do anything."
- "Women can have it all."

And we heard them loud and clear.
But somewhere along the way, we translated those promises into pressure:
- We have to do everything.
- We have to have it all—and prove we're grateful for it.

So we set out to succeed—not just to *do it*, but to *crush it*. Lead the meetings. Raise the kids. Run the household. Stay in shape. Look put-together. Be agreeable. Never drop a ball. And don't forget to smile.

We told ourselves we could win in a man's world...and still get home in time to make dinner. We became the girls who didn't just dream big—we cleaned up after it too.

We were the girls who could do it all...and were quietly breaking because of it.

The cracks didn't form because we weren't strong. They formed because we were never meant to carry it all. Not alone. Not silently. And not at the cost of ourselves.

We were sold a version of empowerment that looked like freedom but felt like servitude—an endless to-do list dressed in heels.

Even as opportunities opened up, expectations multiplied. We weren't told to choose between career and family—we were told to dominate both. And if we ever admitted we were tired or overwhelmed, the response wasn't empathy; it was, "Maybe you just need to manage your time better."

So we kept pushing.

This isn't empowerment. It's self-sacrifice with a smile.

Instead of questioning the exhaustion, we internalize it as failure. And the more capable we appear, the more invisible the cost becomes. In society, this pressure shows up in the following ways:

- *Gender Expectations:* We're expected to crush it at work, raise brilliant, well-behaved kids, keep picture-perfect homes, stay in shape, remain pleasant, and never complain.
- *The Hustle Trap:* We live in a culture that glorifies busy. Back-to-back meetings, late-night emails, PTO we

never take. If we're not exhausted, we must not be trying hard enough.
- *Workplace Pressures:* In the office, we're praised for going the extra mile but penalized if we set or enforce boundaries. We're expected to lead like men and nurture like mothers—without missing a beat.
- *Social Media's Highlight Reel:* If we scroll our feeds, we'll see it: women who make it all look effortless—thriving careers, flawless families, self-care routines that could be magazine spreads. But behind every filtered square is the same pressure to perform, prove, and keep up appearances.

The result? A "do it all" generation of women drowning in impossible expectations, too busy to stop and ask, *At what cost?*

Trauma: The Invisible Driver Behind Overachievement

Trauma results from an incident, series of events, or set of circumstances that an individual experiences as physically or emotionally harmful or threatening. These experiences disrupt our sense of safety, stability, and self—often in ways we may not fully recognize until much later.

Trauma is not just about what happens to you; it's about the lasting imprint those experiences leave behind, including adverse effects on your mental, emotional, physical, and social well-being. And it's far more common than most people realize: Based on a statistic from the National Library of Medicine (see https://www.ncbi.nlm.nih.gov/books/NBK207192/), an estimated 70 percent of adults have experienced a traumatic event at least once in their lives.

Sometimes trauma is a single catastrophic event. More often, it's not. Sometimes it's subtle, cumulative, and invisible. But it leaves a mark all the same.

There's big "T" trauma—the obvious, life-altering experiences: abuse, abandonment, assault, loss. The kind that shakes your foundation and rewires your nervous system to stay on high alert.

And then there's little "t" trauma—the smaller, quieter wounds that build over time: the emotional needs that were never met, the affection that was withheld, the moments you needed comfort and got criticism instead. Trauma isn't always about what happened. Sometimes it's about what *didn't* happen.

You weren't comforted. You weren't protected. You weren't seen.

> **An estimated 70 percent of adults have experienced a traumatic event at least once in their lives.**

Often, high-achieving women are living with trauma that taught the same lessons: *Be better. Do more. Stay in control. Never let them see you struggle.*

Whether big or small, personal trauma experiences create hypervigilant achievers who cling to control, chase perfection, and avoid vulnerability at all costs. Micro-traumas also leave their mark. The constant drip of bias, dismissiveness, and impossible double standards—in classrooms, boardrooms, and even our own homes—conditions women to overdeliver and overperform just to be taken seriously. As a result, overachievement becomes armor. Busyness becomes a shield. Slowing down feels unsafe, because stillness makes space for everything we've worked so hard to bury.

For years, we didn't talk about any of this. It wasn't acceptable. It was taboo to name these things out loud, so we suppressed them. But suppressed doesn't mean gone. Rather, it lives in the way we grind, push, and perform—long after the danger has passed.

The Hardest Things to Let Go of Are the Things That Make You Successful

Here's the uncomfortable truth most people don't talk about: The very habits, traits, and coping mechanisms that got you where you are, are often the ones that keep you stuck.

One of my strongest trauma responses was hypervigilance—always scanning for danger, always preparing for the worst, always on high alert.

In corporate life it was one of the things that made me successful. My job was to safeguard the company from risk. But I didn't just *do* that; I *was* that. The person who caught what others missed. The one who thought ten steps ahead. The one who anticipated problems before they showed up on anyone else's radar.

I was rewarded for it. Promoted for it. Valued for it.

But here's what I didn't see: Hypervigilance wasn't a skill I learned in school. It was a survival instinct that had been running the show long before I ever stepped into a boardroom. It came naturally to me.

And the problem with hypervigilance? You can't just turn it off. It becomes who you are—at work, in motherhood, friendships, relationships, and how you move through the world. I didn't understand that until years later, when I finally started to heal. Only then could I look back and see the pattern.

My trauma responses made me successful in business. Hypervigilance meant I was excellent at risk management and protecting the business. Perfectionism earned me promotions, accolades, and trust. Overfunctioning made me the go-to person who could handle anything without breaking. And my tendency toward people-pleasing built relationships and got me invited into rooms I might not have entered otherwise.

But here's the flip side: What got me ahead also kept me trapped.

Hypervigilance turned into anxiety I couldn't turn off.

Perfectionism became a prison.

Overfunctioning led to burnout.

People-pleasing diluted my voice and masked my true power.

Letting go of these habits wasn't just hard; it felt unnatural. Because for years, they *worked*. They kept me safe, they earned me approval, they helped me rise.

But these trauma-responses-turned-habits also keep us small, exhausted, and disconnected from who we really are. The question isn't whether these patterns have served us. The question is, Are they serving us now? Or are they costing us the very freedom and fulfillment we're working so hard to find?

The hardest shift you'll make isn't changing what you do; it's challenging who you think you need to be. But on the

CHAPTER 4

other side of that? That's where real leadership—and real power—lives.

Sometimes what looks like excellence is really just a well-disguised defense mechanism.

> ## KEY CONCEPT: THE ARRIVAL FALLACY
>
> The Arrival Fallacy is the false belief that once you achieve a specific goal, you will finally feel happy, fulfilled, or "enough." High achievers often chase milestone after milestone, only to find that contentment remains out of reach.
>
> **Exercise**
> Think of the last big goal you achieved, the last big purchase you made. Did it bring the fulfillment you expected? Journal for five minutes on what you were really hoping it would solve.

Where Does Your Never-Enough Story Come From?

Before you can break the Never-Enough Cycle, you need to know who wrote the script.

As you consider the following statements, mark the ones that relate to you.

Childhood Conditioning: The Original Blueprint
- I was praised only when I achieved or succeeded.
- Mistakes weren't allowed or were met with criticism.

- I learned early on to take care of others' needs before my own.
- I still feel uncomfortable asking for help.
- I fear disappointing people more than I fear burning out.

Societal Conditioning: The External Cage
- I feel guilty when I rest.
- I believe I should be able to "do it all."
- I feel pressure to appear flawless—at work, at home, and in public.
- I compare myself to the "perfect" women I see online or in the media.
- I often feel like I'm falling short, even when others praise me.

Trauma Responses: The Invisible Drivers
- I overwork or overachieve to feel safe.
- Slowing down makes me anxious or uncomfortable.
- I feel like if I stop performing, everything will fall apart.
- I don't trust that I'm enough without constant action or accomplishment.
- Deep down, I worry people will leave if I'm not useful.

Your Results: What's Driving Your Never-Enough Cycle
If you checked most of the statements in Childhood Conditioning:

CHAPTER 4

You've been carrying inherited scripts for decades. It's time to stop living by someone else's rules and rewrite who you are and what you deserve.

If you checked most of the statements in Societal Conditioning:

You're drowning in external pressure. You've been trained to measure yourself against impossible standards—and it's time to question *every single one of them*.

If you checked most of the statements in Trauma Responses:

You've been operating in survival mode—but you're safe now. It's time to stop running and start choosing from alignment, not fear.

• • •

You can't break free from what you won't name. PowerShifters name it, call it out, and cut the cord.

And here's the truth: Most women don't check just one box or even one section. We check them all. Because this conditioning is layered. Cumulative. Reinforced from every angle—home, society, and lived experience.

So if you recognize yourself in all three categories, you're not broken. You're conditioned. And now that you've named it, you don't have to be stuck there.

We've been taught to chase success by doing more—perform harder, carry more, push through.

But the cost of that conditioning is *you*: your energy, your peace, your clarity, your identity.

You can't keep living in survival mode and expect to feel fulfilled.

You can't perform your way to peace.

You can't keep proving your worth and expect to live in your power.

Something has to shift—and it starts at the root.

Before we talk about how to break the cycle through Radical Prioritization, you need to understand a deeper truth.

> **You can't break free from what you won't name. PowerShifters name it, call it out, and cut the cord.**

We were taught to hustle harder. To earn our worth through output, perfection, and performance. But growth doesn't come from force; it comes from alignment. That's the foundation of the Ascension Principle.

The Ascension Principle is the belief that your highest impact doesn't come from doing more—it comes from aligning deeper. It's a four-stage framework for intentional elevation:

CHAPTER 4

Clarity → Release → Align → Rise

When you become clear on who you are, release what no longer serves you, and take aligned action, you create success that's sustainable, fulfilling, and fully yours.

It's not about doing more. It's about doing what matters most—in the right order, and from the inside out.

Here's how the Ascension Principle works:

1. Clarity: This is where everything begins. When you're clear on who you are, what you value, and what actually matters to you, you stop chasing and start choosing. Clarity is the foundation for all aligned action. Without it, you default to overfunctioning and people-pleasing.
2. Release: Once you're clear, the next step is shedding what no longer serves you. Old beliefs. Unnecessary obligations. Misaligned expectations. You can't rise if you're weighed down by what was never yours to carry.
3. Align: Alignment is where clarity becomes action. It's when your values, energy, boundaries, and decisions all speak the same language. You stop reacting and start leading. You become intentional...and powerful.
4. Rise: This is the result. When clarity, release, and alignment are in place, your impact expands naturally. You rise without burnout. You grow without guilt. You create success that actually feels like yours.

This is the real path to elevation. Not through more hustle, but through *deep alignment*.

> **You don't hustle your way to the top. You align your way there.**

You don't hustle your way to the top. You align your way there.

In the chapters ahead, we'll unpack exactly how to unlearn these unhealthy beliefs, rewrite the story, and shift from survival mode into alignment. You'll learn how to stop performing for permission and start choosing from power.

This is where the cycle ends and your PowerShift begins.

CHAPTER 4

The Ascension Principle

ALIGNMENT LIFTS YOU

PART II

RADICAL PRIORITIZATION: IDENTITY FIRST. STRATEGY SECOND.

CHAPTER 5

RADICAL PRIORITIZATION: THE SHIFT THAT CHANGES EVERYTHING

You've felt it, haven't you? The weight you carry without acknowledgment. The pressure to hold everything together, with a smile on your face but exhaustion in your bones. Maybe you've asked yourself, *How did I get here? Why does it all fall on me?*

I've been there too. I know that weight. I know what it feels like to chase success with everything you have—only to wonder, somewhere along the way, if you've lost yourself in the process.

What you'll discover in the pages ahead is how PowerShifters—women like you—stop carrying what isn't theirs and finally take back control. For me, success meant prioritizing what truly mattered and letting go of the relentless pressure to do it all. That shift—breaking free from the constant noise of "more" and stepping into what truly matters—wasn't instant, but it set me on the path to creating something powerful: the *Radical Prioritization Method*. Radical

Prioritization is the art of reclaiming your life by saying no to everything that isn't aligned with your true self.

This book is about a fundamental shift in how we define and live success. It's about embracing a framework for prioritization that isn't about doing more or hustling harder. Radical Prioritization is about doing *less*—but doing it more intentionally, with absolute clarity about your true desires, your values, and the impact you want to have.

> • • • •
> **Radical Prioritization is the art of reclaiming your life by saying no to everything that isn't aligned with your true self.**
> • • • •

For years, I did everything I was *supposed* to do. I checked every box, climbed every ladder, and proved my worth in every room I walked into. I pushed through exhaustion, ignored the warning signs, and convinced myself that this was the price of achievement. That if I could just do *more*, be *more*, maybe—finally—I would feel like it was enough. Like *I* was enough.

But life has a way of forcing you to stop. My body gave out. My daughter was in a hospital bed, fighting to breathe, while I sat there realizing how deeply misaligned I had become. I had spent so much time running toward the next milestone that I had lost sight of what mattered. I knew something had to change.

That's why I wrote this book.

High-achieving women don't need more strategies to optimize their lives—productivity hacks, better efficiency, or simply learning to balance it all. We need a fundamental shift in how we define success in the first place. We need a new framework, one rooted in research, neuroscience, and the lived experiences of women who have been caught in the Never-Enough Cycle for far too long.

Radical Prioritization isn't about sacrificing ambition; it's about reclaiming it. It's about learning how to stop pouring yourself into everything and start focusing on what truly moves the needle for your definition of success, well-being, and fulfillment. This book is about helping you step out of survival mode and into a life where your work, your time, and your energy align with who you *actually* are, not who the world expects you to be.

Most people think they need better time management. But what they really need is Strategic Capacity. **Strategic Capacity is the ability to make bold, aligned decisions—because you've stopped managing time and started managing what actually matters. It's the mental clarity, emotional resilience, and energetic bandwidth to lead, live, and move with intention. Not just more space in your calendar—more power in your presence.**

What Is Radical Prioritization?

Radical Prioritization is a transformative, identity-first approach that helps high-achieving women stop performing success—and start leading from what actually matters. Rooted in neuroscience and guided by values, it's how you reclaim your time, energy, and focus by aligning every decision with who you are, not with who you've had to be.

This isn't about doing more—it's about doing what's **true**. *What stays, what goes, what shifts? You decide.*

That's the power of Radical Prioritization.

Why Is Radical Prioritization Important?

In a world that constantly demands more, women often find themselves overcommitted, undervalued, and disconnected from their own needs. Radical Prioritization offers a clear, actionable framework to recalibrate, ensuring that decisions are made from a place of alignment, not sacrifice. By prioritizing what matters most, women can achieve holistic success—balancing professional achievement with personal fulfillment and reclaiming their power to live authentically and intentionally.

This method is designed to help us stop running in circles and start focusing on what truly matters. We're drowning in distractions, overwhelmed by endless to-do lists, and stuck in a cycle where success feels elusive. The Radical Prioritization Method offers a way out.

It isn't about adding more to your plate. It's about replacing "I have to" with "I choose to." It's about rejecting the idea that busyness equals worth and instead embracing alignment, fulfillment, and purpose. To do that, you need to know what truly matters to you and prioritize accordingly.

I developed the Radical Prioritization framework to help women refocus and realign. My hope is that by the time you turn the last page, you won't just have a set of tools—you'll have permission. Permission to redefine what success looks

CHAPTER 5

like for *you*. Permission to say no without guilt. Permission to stop proving and start *living*.

Because the life you want? The one where you achieve *more* by doing *less*? It's not a distant dream. It starts here. It starts now. And it starts with *you*.

In this journey, I'll draw from my own experiences and the experiences of women I've worked with, and we'll also examine the research findings from my study of high-achieving women. This research offers critical insights into the pressures we face and the invisible costs of this "success at all costs" mindset. Women, more than ever, are reaching a breaking point, and it's time to rebuild from the inside out.

As you turn the pages of this book, know that you are not alone. This is not just my story—this is the story of women everywhere who are hungry for a life of balance, purpose, and sustainable success. It's time to embrace Radical Prioritization and break free from the chains of hustle and urgency that no longer serve us.

KEY CONCEPT: DECISION FATIGUE

Decision fatigue is the decline in quality decision-making after a long period of making choices. The more decisions you make in a day, the more mentally depleted you become, leading to poor prioritization and reactive choices. Our impact multiplies when we stop carrying what's not ours. This isn't about small moves. We create space for what matters.

Exercise
1. Write down three things you're doing right now that dilute your energy.
2. Cross one off permanently. Decide what you'll amplify with the energy you get back.
3. Identify one current commitment or project that's draining you without impact. Now identify one that could create exponential impact if given more energy. Shift your focus accordingly.

The Excuses That Keep You Stuck (and Why They Sound So Convincing)

Before we go deeper, I want to make one thing clear (and this might sting): At some point, you're going to encounter internal resistance, if you haven't already. You're going to tell yourself...

I don't have the time to...

I'm not good at...

I'm not smart/confident/pretty/talented enough to...

It's not the right time.

Sound familiar? I've heard them all. I've *used* them all.

These are not just excuses—they're shields. They help us avoid discomfort, dodge decisions, and stay in motion without truly moving forward. They feel safe.

But staying behind "I'm too busy" is just another form of settling. So I'm going to lovingly call you out right now: You're

CHAPTER 5

> Shift happens when you stop waiting for answers—and start trusting your own.
>
> When we first began working together, Tonya described herself as unconfident, restless, and full of self-doubt. Like many high-achieving women, she had mastered the external game—meeting deadlines, climbing ladders, playing the part—but inside, she was questioning everything. She was expecting another checklist. A road map. A fix.
>
> But instead of giving her answers, I asked her better questions. Questions that challenged her to pause long enough to hear her own voice. Through that process, she realized something powerful: She didn't need permission or a prescription—she needed alignment.
>
> The transformation didn't come from doing more. It came from doing the right things, the ones that aligned with her values and truth. She learned to trust herself in moments of doubt, root her decisions in her nonnegotiables, and lead from her center.
>
> By the end of our work, she no longer felt like she was chasing clarity. She was living it—confident, grounded, and empowered. Because the most powerful form of prioritization isn't external. It's internal.

not too busy. You're just too accustomed to putting yourself last.

And that stops here.

Shift happens when you finally say, "I'm done settling."

Pause here and write down every reason you've given yourself for not making a shift. Look at each one and ask yourself, *Is this a truth...or a story? What is it costing me to keep believing it?*

Why Change Feels So Hard (and Why You Avoid It)

Before you start blaming yourself for procrastinating or "lacking discipline," let's get something straight: Change is hard for every human—not because we're lazy, but because we're wired for safety.

Here's what's really going on under the surface:

There's comfort in the known—even when it's painful.

You might hate the overpacked calendar, the stress, the resentment, the chaos. But you know it. It's familiar. Your brain would rather stay in discomfort it understands than step into the unknown.

Fear of the unknown is real.

Change threatens the ego, the identity you've worked so hard to build. Even if that identity is exhausting you, your brain will cling to it. It whispers, *But who will you be without this?*

Your brain needs rewiring—and it's not as scary as it sounds.

You've spent years reinforcing certain thought patterns: *Prove. Perform. Please. Repeat.* Changing that wiring takes intentional practice—but it's absolutely possible.

CHAPTER 5

You're addicted to your own stress hormones.
Cortisol and adrenaline become a chemical cocktail your body runs on—they become fuel. You think you're running on energy, but really, you're running on stress. That high is hard to quit.

You have to find your new normal.
Stillness feels foreign when you've been running on overdrive. The first time you slow down, it will feel uncomfortable, almost like something's wrong. That's the beginning of alignment. With practice, peace becomes your new baseline.

> **You're not too busy. You're just too accustomed to putting yourself last.**

• • •

Change doesn't just ask you to do something differently. It requires you to become someone different.

Who You Were, Who You Are, and Who You Are Becoming

Radical Prioritization isn't just a time-management strategy; it's a transformational framework that requires you to go beyond the surface of daily tasks and examine the deeper questions of identity, purpose, and growth. It requires clarity, courage, and intentionality. It's a process that moves you from living by default to living on purpose—and it begins by answering these questions:

- Who was I, and what stories did I carry with me?
- Who am I today, and how can I show up as my authentic self?
- Who am I becoming, and how can my priorities now create that future?

Let's look more closely and take time to reflect on these three crucial layers of your life.

1. *Who You Were*
This reflection involves looking back at the person you once were—the versions of yourself shaped by past experiences, stories, and identities. Who did you think you needed to be? What were the expectations placed on you? What roles or responsibilities did you take on because you thought it was part of who you *had to* be? Perhaps you were the overachiever, the caretaker, the perfectionist, or the silent sufferer. Understanding this phase helps you recognize the stories that shaped your decisions and actions—and how they might no longer serve you.

Key Questions to Reflect On
- What story am I living right now?
- What beliefs or behaviors from my past are still influencing my decisions today?
- How did I define success, fulfillment, and worth back then?
- How has my past shaped the stories I tell myself now?

2. Who You Are

This is the present moment, when Radical Prioritization comes into play. It's a chance to reflect on the person you are today—the version of yourself that's shaped by your current experiences, values, and choices. Who are you, right now, in this very moment? What do you value most in your life? This phase calls for honesty and introspection. It's about acknowledging how far you've come and confronting what's no longer serving you.

Key Questions to Reflect On
- Who am I beyond the stories I've been told?
- What aspects of my current life align with who I want to be?
- What does success look like for me right now?
- What do I value most in this moment, and how am I living those values?

3. Who You Are Becoming

This is the most exciting and transformative part of the equation—the version of yourself you are stepping into. Radical Prioritization isn't just about managing the present moment; it's about creating space for who you are becoming. It requires you to envision your future self—the person you want to be in five, ten, and twenty years. It's about setting intentions, redefining success, and charting the course for growth, expansion, and purpose. Who do you want to become, and how can your priorities today help you step into that future? The priorities you choose become the behaviors you model—for your team, your family, and everyone watching.

Key Questions to Reflect On
- Who do I want to be?
- What kind of legacy do I want to leave behind?
- How do I envision my life in the future?
- What values and actions will guide me toward becoming the person I am destined to be?

What Are Values, Really?
Your values aren't a list of nice words you write down once and forget. They are your foundation. They're what guide your decisions when no one's watching. They're the lines you don't cross and the things you fight for without hesitation.

> **Radical Prioritization isn't just about what you do—it's about who you believe yourself to be.**

Values are the nonnegotiables that define *who you are* and *how you lead*. When you're clear on your values, decisions become simpler. You stop agonizing over what to do. You know what's aligned—and what's not—and you act accordingly.

But here's the catch: Most women have never been asked to name their values. We've been taught to adapt, accommodate, and fit into other people's priorities. So if you come up blank when I ask you what matters most, you're not broken—you're conditioned.

CHAPTER 5

How Do You Identify Your Values?
Start by noticing what triggers you—and what lights you up. What makes you furious? What makes you feel most alive? Usually, those emotions point to your values.

If disrespect makes your blood boil, respect is a core value. If being dismissed makes you feel invisible, recognition or truth might be a core value. If you feel most alive when creating, freedom and expression might be core values. Your values aren't what you *think* should matter; they're what already matter—you just haven't named them yet.

Ask yourself:

When do I feel most like me?

What's nonnegotiable in my life?

What am I no longer willing to tolerate?

Where am I out of alignment, and what's the value I've abandoned?

If I were to ask your family, your team, coworkers, or boss what they believe you stand for or represent, what would they say?

Once you know your values, those values become your compass.

Radical Prioritization isn't just about what you do—it's about who you believe yourself to be. That's what we'll explore in the next chapter.

CHAPTER 6

HOW IDENTITY SHAPES YOUR WORLD, YOUR CHOICES, AND YOUR OUTCOMES

Some of us have participated in the awkward icebreaker that asks us to "describe yourself in one word." Every time someone asks me that, I start to sweat. What do I say? *Coach? Mom? Entrepreneur?* No, those are roles. Do I say *ambitious, kind, loving?* So boring.

The truth is, none of those words even scratches the surface. They're labels—and labels are easy. What's underneath them is identity. And identity is everything.

Your identity isn't just the way you describe yourself to other people. It runs much deeper. Identity is the silent script that defines what you believe you deserve, how much space you take up, and how far you allow yourself to go.

If you believe you are the fixer, you'll prioritize solving everyone else's problems over your own needs. You'll say yes when you want to say no, because it reinforces the belief that your value lies in usefulness.

If you believe you are worthy only when achieving, you'll overcommit, burn out...and still question your value. You'll chase gold stars and external validation long after they've lost meaning.

If you believe your worth depends on being needed, you'll struggle to set boundaries and wear resentment like a second skin. You'll become the woman who carries everyone and silently wonders why no one ever carries her.

Identity is the filter through which you interpret every situation. Rejection doesn't just sting; it confirms the story that you're not enough. Praise doesn't just feel good; it becomes a drug you crave.

And ultimately, identity determines outcomes. Every decision—what you pursue, what you tolerate, what you invest in—flows from who you believe you are. If your identity is built on survival, you'll prioritize from fear. If your identity is built on ownership and alignment, you'll prioritize with power.

When you shift your identity from *performer* to *creator*, from *prover* to *owner*, from *caretaker* to *leader*, the lens through which you view the world changes. You stop asking, What will they think? and start asking, What do I want to build? You shift from reaction to intention. From busyness to bold, focused action. From proving to choosing.

Because your identity isn't just who you are—it's the foundation for what you allow yourself to become. Your thoughts create neural pathways that trigger emotional responses, and those emotions drive your behaviors. When your identity is built on outdated survival patterns (as we explored in chapter 2), your brain reinforces them through repeated thoughts

CHAPTER 6

and emotional loops. But when you rewire those thoughts, when you choose to believe new stories about who you are, you change your emotional state and, over time, your actions, habits, and outcomes. Identity work is brain work, and it reshapes your reality from the inside out.

If you don't change your identity, you won't change your priorities. If you don't question the story you've been given, it will run your life.

As we've discussed, our priorities aren't random. We don't just wake up one day and decide to overcommit, overwork, or oversacrifice. We are conditioned into it. The stories we carry—about success, about worth, about what we *owe*—dictate what we say yes to, what we tolerate, and what we sacrifice.

Looking back, I can see it clearly: I was always someone who stepped up, who took responsibility, who made things happen.

In elementary school, I proudly wore the bright orange safety patrol belt, guiding others, making sure everyone got in and out of school safely, and taking ownership of things bigger than myself.

In high school, I found myself leading again as part of the student council. Organizing, planning—not because I had to, but because it felt natural to create structure and support the people around me.

In college, I was a campus tour guide—the first face prospective students met, the person they trusted to show them what was possible. I didn't just point the way; I carried the weight of representing something bigger.

Those moments weren't random. They were early signs of who I was: someone who leads, nurtures, protects, and makes others feel safe and capable. But over time, I started to realize something: The strength that served me so well could also turn into pressure. Responsibility became expectation. Leadership became performance.

> **When you rewrite the narrative, your priorities shift effortlessly.**

My challenge wasn't simply to stop leading. It was to lead from authenticity, not obligation. To own my natural gifts without letting them own me.

Rewriting Your Story

Every strength has a shadow. Leadership without boundaries becomes martyrdom. Responsibility without rest becomes resentment. The desire to guide and protect can slowly turn into the need to control and overfunction.

I've learned that the work isn't to abandon these parts of myself—they're part of who I am. The work is to channel them with intention. To let leadership flow from clarity, not conditioning. To offer support without sacrificing myself. To take ownership without carrying weight that isn't mine.

These qualities are burdens when *they* direct *you*. But they are gifts when *you* direct *them*.

When you rewrite the narrative, your priorities shift effortlessly.

For me, rewriting my story meant untangling my worth from achievement. It meant learning that I didn't have to prove my value through exhaustion. It meant letting go of the identity that told me I was only as good as what I could offer others.

When I stopped living in the shadow of my old story, my priorities transformed.
- I started saying no without guilt.
- I stopped sacrificing my well-being for the sake of being *needed*.
- I redefined success not as proving, but as living in alignment.

If your life feels overwhelming, if your priorities feel out of control, if you are caught in the Never-Enough Cycle, ask yourself:
- *What are the pivotal moments in my life that shaped who I am?*
- *Who told me who I needed to be, and when did I start believing them?*
- *What roles do I play out of obligation rather than desire?*
- *What do I believe I have to prove, and to whom?*
- *When was the last time I felt fully myself—no mask, no performance? Where was I, and who was I with?*
- *If I stripped away titles, achievements, and expectations, what's left?*
- *What's one belief about my worth that no longer serves me?*
- *If my younger self could see who I am now, what would she celebrate? What would she question?*
- *What parts of my identity are rooted in survival rather than choice? Am I ready to release them?*
- *What identity am I afraid of letting go of?*

Shift happens—usually after one meltdown and a glass of wine.

The sooner you let go of the old story, the sooner you can start living the life you want.

> ## KEY CONCEPT: IDENTITY-BASED DECISION-MAKING
>
> Identity-based decision-making is the process of making choices based on who you *want* to become rather than who you've been. Instead of making decisions out of habit or obligation, women must align their choices with their future, evolved selves. PowerShifters understand that the stories we internalize about our worth, our capabilities, and our potential are not the full truth of who we are.
>
> **Exercise**
> Who are you *beyond* the stories you've been told? Do any of these stories resonate with you? Think about what it would look like to strip away the layers of *shoulds* and *musts* to see yourself in a clearer light.

Unmasking the Real You

Most high-achieving women don't just work hard—they *perform* identities that were never theirs to begin with.

We call it ambition. Drive. Dedication. But what's often underneath? Survival.

The truth is, many of us learned early that being ourselves wasn't safe enough, acceptable enough, or lovable enough.

CHAPTER 6

So we adapted. We shape-shifted. We learned to play roles that made everyone else comfortable—even if they made us unrecognizable to ourselves.

And those roles got rewarded. So we kept playing them.

These aren't flaws. They're coping mechanisms. Brilliant, strategic, and—at some point—necessary. But now? They're the very patterns keeping us stuck in burnout, misalignment, and emotional exhaustion.

In my research and coaching work, five dominant patterns consistently show up in high-achieving women who are caught in the Never-Enough Cycle. I call them the Overfunctioning Archetypes:

- **The Fixer**

  You solve everyone else's problems, often before they ask. You feel responsible for holding everything together, and your worth is tied to being the one who comes through—even when it costs you.

- **The Rescuer**

  You overextend emotionally. You carry the weight of other people's pain, needs, and decisions. You're the strong one, the supportive one—and the one no one checks on.

- **The Prover**

  You chase validation through achievement. Nothing ever feels like "enough" because you've built your identity on performance. You feel valuable only when you're producing, achieving, or winning.

- **The Peacemaker**

  You avoid conflict like it's a fire. You minimize your

needs to keep the peace, often silencing your truth to stay agreeable, likable, or easy to love.

- **The Chameleon**
You read the room and become who you think others want you to be. You're adaptable, high-functioning, and outwardly successful—but inside, you've lost sight of who you actually are.

These archetypes are masks—learned roles we put on to feel safe, accepted, and needed. But here's the thing: What kept you safe is now keeping you stuck.

Until you name the identity that's been driving you, you can't choose a new one.

So I'll ask you this: *Which one feels a little too familiar?*

These masks made you successful. They've also made you exhausted. You are not the role. You are not the mask. You are the woman beneath it—ready to reclaim her voice, her worth, and her life.

• • • •

What kept you safe is now keeping you stuck.

• • • •

PowerShifters learn to name the truth they've been avoiding—because that's where the real shift happens. We call this the *Say the Hard Thing* moment. It's the exact second you stop protecting everyone else's comfort and start protecting your own truth. Whether it's a conversation with your partner, your boss, or yourself—there is always one hard thing you're avoiding that could change everything.

CHAPTER 6

What's one truth you've been avoiding—about your capacity, your career, your relationship, your happiness, or yourself?

Write it down. Say it out loud. *Because the shift doesn't start when you plan—it starts when you say the hard thing.*

PowerShifters rewrite the script—on their terms.

Turn the page. Let's start living from there.

• • • •

PowerShifters rewrite the script— on their terms.

• • • •

CHAPTER 7

STOP PRETENDING, START LIVING

Now that you've dismantled the old script, it's time to create a new foundation. The next step is aligning your priorities with your values, not your conditioning. I call this anchoring into authenticity. When your values become your compass, prioritization stops feeling like a battle and starts feeling like freedom. As we explored in chapter 5, your values are not a list of *shoulds*—they are your blueprint. PowerShifters build everything on that foundation.

From the outside, reinvention looks like a bold leap—a fearless transformation into a truer, stronger version of yourself. But the reality? It's often born from crisis. My own reinvention wasn't a strategic, carefully planned journey. It was survival. A reckoning. Not only did my upbringing shape who I am today, but the stories I told myself about who I was—and more importantly, who I was *not*—dictated my journey for years.

Your values are not a list of *shoulds*—they are your blueprint.

Before you can align with who you are, you need to untangle who you had to become to feel safe. That girl who twisted herself into knots wasn't weak—she was surviving. But now, you get to choose from a place of power, not protection.

This is where the real work begins.

- Where in your life have you looked for answers outside of yourself? What did you hope to find, and did it give you the clarity or validation you were seeking?
- Can you think of a time when you ignored your gut instinct? What happened, and what did it teach you about trusting yourself?
- How were you taught—directly or indirectly—to silence your own needs, feelings, or intuition? Who or what influenced the belief that others knew better than you?
- If your inner voice could speak to you right now, what would she say? What does she need you to hear?
- What is one small way you can start rebuilding trust with yourself today? How can you listen to yourself without seeking external validation first?

The Stories That Wrote Me

I once mistook control and manipulation for love—because it looked like protection and felt like safety. I was too young to know the difference. I learned to scan faces for approval, to shape-shift into whatever version of me the moment required. I became a chameleon—blending, performing, bending—just to belong, just to be enough.

At a young age, you don't question things. You just adapt.

CHAPTER 7

But with every mask I put on, I moved further away from myself. I didn't ask what I wanted, what I valued, or who I really was. I only asked, Who do they need me to be?

It would take me years—and a lot of unlearning—to realize that constantly contorting yourself for others is the fastest way to lose your voice, your boundaries, and your soul.

Most women go through a phase like this—people-pleasing, adapting, learning to shrink parts of themselves to fit in. Many outgrow it—for the most part. But for me, it didn't feel like a phase. It was who I needed to be to feel safe, accepted, and valued. That chameleon behavior wasn't just about adaptability—it was a trauma response known as fawning. Fawning refers to consistently abandoning your own needs to serve others to avoid conflict, criticism, or disapproval. It's the most socially acceptable survival mechanism—but also the most self-erasing (see https://psychcentral.com/health/fawn-response#definition).

By the time I reached adulthood, I didn't know what I liked. I didn't know what I wanted. I knew only how to excel, how to serve, how to prove. I knew only what I was told I "should" like and want. I never stopped to ask myself simple questions: *What brings me joy? What do I need? What do I believe in?* My worth had always been measured by how well I pleased others, not by how well I knew myself.

That conditioning seeped into every corner of my life—every decision, every relationship, every moment that I stayed small to feel safe. I wasn't living. I was performing.

The day I realized this was the day it hit me: I could keep following the script that manipulation and fear had handed me—or I could burn it and write a new one. One built on truth, autonomy, and self-respect.

Though this part of my past shaped my journey, it does not define me. It's through the ongoing process of healing, reflection, and redefining my identity that I've been able to transform these once-limiting beliefs into sources of strength. The girl who learned to earn love is gone. The woman now standing here knows she's worthy of it without conditions.

According to my research, 61 percent of working women report feeling pressure to be perfect (e.g., perfect mother, wife, employee)—a relentless demand that leads to emotional exhaustion and deep misalignment with their true selves. We live in a world that celebrates our external success but rarely asks if that success feels *right* to us.

> • • • •
> **Sixty-one percent of working women report feeling pressure to be perfect.**
> • • • •

For most of my life, I didn't question the beliefs I carried about myself—I just accepted them as truth. I believed that I had to work harder than everyone else to be taken seriously. That my worth was measured by my productivity. That saying no would make me unlikable. That success meant sacrifice. I never stopped to wonder where those beliefs came from.

The truth is, so many of the stories we tell ourselves—about who we are, what we're capable of, and what we deserve—*aren't actually ours*. They were handed to us by family, culture, society,

CHAPTER 7

and past experiences. We inherited them from the expectations placed on us as children, from the way love and approval were given (or withheld), from conditioning that rewarded self-sacrifice and discouraged self-trust. And over time, these beliefs became so deeply ingrained that we mistook them for facts rather than conditioned patterns.

But not all these stories are loud. Some live in the quiet moments, the ones we'd rather forget or explain away.

At age twenty-three, I said yes when I meant no. Not to a job or a project, but to a man. I got engaged because I thought that's what I was supposed to do. Because I believed he loved me. Because I didn't want to disappoint him. Because I didn't want to be the woman who walked away from something every woman dreamed of. I convinced myself this was what love looked like. But deep down, I knew.

> **A belief is not a truth—it's just a thought you've repeated enough times to accept as reality. And that means it can be unlearned.**

So one day, I finally mustered up the courage to leave. I packed my life into garbage bags and walked out. That was my first real lesson in self-betrayal—and in reclaiming my voice.

Because when you're conditioned to keep the peace, perform to perfection, and avoid disappointing others, walking away feels like failure.

But it's not. It's freedom.

I didn't have language for it at the time. But looking back, that moment was the beginning of unlearning everything I'd been taught about who I needed to be to be loved.

A belief is not a truth—it's just a thought you've repeated enough times to accept as reality. And that means it can be unlearned.

The Stories We Tell Ourselves

We all carry stories, silent scripts that run beneath the surface and shape every choice we make. As we've discussed, most of them aren't true. But we live by them anyway. These myths become our inner dialogue. They sound like logic, but they're actually conditioning. They sound like ambition, but they're often fear.

Read the following statements and mark each one that feels familiar. These are the stories shaping your reality, whether you realize it or not.

Success and Ambition
- "I have to work twice as hard to be taken seriously."
- "If I slow down, I'll fall behind."
- "I can't be successful and have a balanced life."
- "I'm not leadership material."
- "People like me don't get opportunities like that."
- "I'm not ready yet. I need another degree, certification, or more experience."

CHAPTER 7

Self-Worth and Identity
- "I should be grateful for what I have. Wanting more is selfish."
- "I'm not the kind of person who takes big risks."
- "If I stand up for myself, people will think I'm difficult."
- "I'm too much."
- "I'm not enough."
- "I don't have anything special to offer."
- "Other people have real talent. I just got lucky."

Money and Financial Independence
- "I'm not good with money."
- "Making a lot of money would change who I am."
- "Wealthy women are greedy or selfish."
- "I don't deserve financial abundance."
- "If I earn more than my partner, it will create problems."
- "I could never charge that much for my work."

Relationships and Motherhood
- "I have to put others first or I'm a bad partner/mother/daughter."
- "If I take time for myself, I'm being selfish."
- "I have to do it all. No one else will step up."
- "Good mothers sacrifice everything for their kids."
- "If I set boundaries, I'll push people away."
- "Love means proving my worth over and over."

Body and Appearance
- "I'll be happy when I lose weight."

- "I don't look the part, so I won't be taken seriously."
- "I'm too old to start something new."
- "I have to be perfect to be accepted."
- "I have to look flawless."
- "People will value me only if I'm attractive."

Confidence and Visibility
- "I hate being the center of attention."
- "What if I fail in front of everyone?"
- "I don't belong in those rooms."
- "If I share my true thoughts, people will judge me."
- "Who am I to think I can do this?"
- "I'll start when I feel more confident."

Time and Productivity
- "I don't have time to focus on myself."
- "If I rest, I'm being lazy."
- "Busyness equals worth."
- "Everything will fall apart if I stop juggling all the things."
- "I can't afford to slow down."

Change and Reinvention
- "It's too late to start over."
- "I've invested too much to walk away now."
- "This is just how life is—why fight it?"
- "I don't know who I am outside of my job/relationship/motherhood."
- "People like me don't get second chances."

CHAPTER 7

Look at the statements you marked. Also consider any statements you make to yourself that are not on this list.

Now ask yourself:

Are these beliefs I carry about myself truly mine? Or were they passed down to me, shaped by the fears, limitations, or expectations of others?

Do they align with the person I want to become? Or are they keeping me stuck in an outdated version of myself?

Reclaiming Your Story

The moment you recognize that a belief was *given* to you, you also recognize that you have the power to let it go. You are not bound by someone else's version of who you should be. You get to decide what is true for you now.

When we live out of sync with our values and true needs, we experience what psychologists call *cognitive dissonance*—the psychological stress that arises when our actions contradict our internal beliefs. For women, this misalignment often presents as:

- People-pleasing disguised as ambition
- Overachievement as a form of self-worth
- A fear of stillness, because it forces us to confront what's missing

I didn't just experience this in my early years; I carried it into my corporate life, climbing the ladder with a relentless hunger to prove myself. It took burnout to make me see it. It took reinvention to make me change it.

The Power of Listening to Yourself

Women are resourceful. When stress builds or life gets heavy, we reach for the things that give us a sense of relief—a break, a breath, a moment to ourselves. For some, it's a long walk, a hot bath, or watching a good show. For others, it's journaling, painting, cooking, reading, or meditating. Some lace up their sneakers and hit the gym. Others pour a glass of wine and scroll through social media. Some just sit in their car because it's all they have the energy for.

These coping strategies—in all their forms—aren't wrong. In fact, they're deeply human. They give us short-term relief, emotional release, even moments of joy. But here's the thing most of us aren't saying out loud:

Self-care is not a cure.

It's a Band-Aid—a necessary one, yes—but a temporary fix for a deeper misalignment.

Because no matter how much you walk, stretch, journal, paint, pray, scroll, run, or rest, it won't fully work if you're not listening. You'll be soothing the symptoms but ignoring the source.

And that was me, for a long time.

I am, unapologetically, a wellness junkie. Over the years, I've tried nearly every healing modality out there. All of it. And while each tool offered something valuable, none of it truly shifted me until I learned to listen—not to the experts or the protocols, but to *myself*.

Because the body keeps score, but it also speaks.

And healing isn't about doing more. It's about *hearing* more.

CHAPTER 7

It's about recognizing that your exhaustion, your migraines, your irritability, your inability to slow down—those aren't random. They're signals. And if you keep treating the symptoms without addressing the root, you'll stay stuck in a cycle of temporary relief and chronic misalignment.

The breakthrough didn't come from the practices themselves. It came from the pause between them. The space where I finally asked, *What is my body trying to tell me that I've been too busy to hear?*

That's when healing began.

Over the years, I've explored countless wellness and healing modalities in my quest to restore balance and reclaim my health. I've found value in many of them, each offering something unique, helping me to reconnect with myself, release old patterns, and heal from both physical and emotional stress. These practices became part of my tool kit, and through them, I was able to tap into my body's wisdom in ways I hadn't been able to before.

I turned to breathwork, which taught me how to slow down, calm my racing mind, and activate the parasympathetic nervous system—inviting relaxation and clarity back into my life. Emotional Freedom Technique (EFT), or tapping, became a powerful tool to release stuck emotions, using acupressure points to help my body process trauma and anxiety. Somatic exercises helped me reconnect with my body, releasing tension that had accumulated over years of neglecting my own needs in service of others.

There were also therapies such as EMDR (eye movement desensitization and reprocessing) that guided me through reprocessing trauma, shifting negative thought patterns, and rewiring my brain's response to stress. Cognitive behavioral therapy (CBT) offered practical tools for managing my mindset and reframing my thoughts, while vagus nerve stimulation became a helpful method for calming my nervous system, bringing me back to a place of balance. Nervous system regulation exercises helped me stay grounded and present.

I also embraced alternative physical therapies—infrared saunas, red light therapy, and PEMF mats—to nurture my body on a cellular level. Each of these practices made a difference, offering relief, relaxation, and even moments of profound healing.

But here's the thing: No matter how many modalities I tried or how many tools I added to my collection, what made the biggest difference was listening to myself.

None of these practices would have been effective if I hadn't learned to tune in to my body, my feelings, and my inner voice. The real shift came when I stopped relying solely on external solutions and began to recognize that my body already knew what it needed. It was not about "fixing" something that was broken but rather about honoring what I was feeling, paying attention to the signals my body was sending, and responding with compassion and care.

Listening to myself meant finally getting quiet enough to hear the truth of what was going on inside—recognizing the deep exhaustion I had been masking, acknowledging the emotions I had been suppressing, and understanding that healing was not about doing more but about allowing space for what needed to be felt, released, and nurtured.

CHAPTER 7

Breathwork didn't work until I allowed myself to feel the emotions I had been pushing down. EFT tapping wasn't as effective until I gave myself permission to let go of guilt for needing help. Somatic exercises brought me healing only when I connected to my body's subtle cues instead of dismissing them as unimportant. I found true healing when I began to honor the wisdom within me—when I became still enough to hear my own voice.

KEY CONCEPT: SOMATIC INTELLIGENCE

The body's ability to store and communicate stress, trauma, and emotions is called somatic intelligence. Many high achievers intellectualize their struggles but ignore the physical symptoms (chronic tension, migraines, exhaustion) that are trying to signal misalignment. PowerShifters don't drift; they lead from alignment. It's not about pleasing the world. It's about anchoring into what matters.

Exercise
Write down your top five values—*without* overthinking. Now audit the past two weeks. How well does your time reflect those values? What's the biggest misalignment?

Authenticity as a Radical Act

Authenticity isn't just about "being yourself." It's about *choosing yourself* in a world that constantly demands otherwise. It means redefining success on your own terms rather than measuring it by external expectations. It's about reclaiming the parts of you that have been buried under obligation, survival, or the belief that you have to be more in order to be enough.

And yet most women struggle to make this shift. Through my work with women leaders, consistent patterns emerge around why they feel so disconnected:

- Fear of judgment (*What if people don't accept the real me?*)
- Guilt for wanting more (*What if I disappoint those who rely on me?*)
- Uncertainty about what authenticity even looks like (*Who am I if I strip away the expectations?*)

These fears are valid. But they are not permanent.

Realignment doesn't happen all at once. It happens in micro-decisions, in quiet moments of courage. It happens when we start asking:

What do I truly want?

What am I no longer willing to tolerate?

Who am I when I stop performing?

The goal is not to abandon ambition or success—it's to align those things with who you are. When you root into your authenticity, you don't lose your drive; you channel it in a way that nourishes rather than depletes you.

The journey back to yourself is not about becoming someone new. It's about *returning* to who you were before the world told you who to be.

CHAPTER 8

BUSYNESS BREAKS YOU— ALIGN YOUR ACTIONS

For me, one of the most profound lessons on priorities came in a dimly lit hospital room, holding my father's hand (the man who raised me) as he took his final breaths. I was eight months pregnant with my second daughter—carrying life while watching life slip away. And in those moments, everything that once seemed urgent—the meetings, the deadlines, the endless attempts to prove my worth—vanished.

And with this came clarity: Time is our most precious, nonrenewable resource. And how we choose to spend it defines not only our lives but the legacy we leave behind.

We live with the illusion that we have time, that we can circle back to what matters after the next project, the next promotion, the next crisis. But life doesn't wait. It doesn't pause for us to finally prioritize what's important. It forces us to confront it—often when it's too late.

In that hospital room, I wasn't thinking about what I had accomplished. I was thinking about the conversations I didn't have, the moments I missed, the connections I delayed. I realized that priorities aren't written in planners or checked off lists. They are etched into how we live, moment by moment.

Perhaps you've been doing so much. But are you doing what matters? PowerShifters know the difference and make the call.

> • • • •
> **Either you choose your priorities or life will choose them for you.**
> • • • •

Most women are taught that choosing themselves is selfish. That putting their peace, presence, and purpose at the top of the list is indulgent. But that's the conditioning that keeps us exhausted and disconnected.

That day, sitting between life and death, I learned this truth: Either you choose your priorities or life will choose them for you. And if you don't make the choice with intention, you'll end up living someone else's version of success—while missing the moments that truly matter.

Yet for most women, that feels impossible.

The Cost of Living on Autopilot

My research found that 54 percent of working women struggle to disconnect from work. They feel trapped in the cycle of busyness, mistaking movement for progress, productivity for purpose.

The result?

- We give our best energy to things that don't truly matter.

CHAPTER 8

- We say yes out of obligation rather than alignment.
- We delay joy, peace, and fulfillment, waiting for "someday" to arrive.

But *someday* is not a strategy. Clarity is.

Radical Prioritization isn't about doing more efficiently—it's about *choosing differently*. It's about redirecting our time, energy, and focus toward what is important to us instead of what we've been conditioned to believe is urgent.

Shift happens when you drop the guilt and pick up what actually matters.

Disrupt

You can't shift what you won't name. This step exposes the patterns, identities, and inherited expectations that have shaped how you move through the world. You'll get honest about who you are at your core and the values that are inherently important to you.

This is where you stop confusing your worth with your output.

Redefine

Once you're anchored in authenticity, it's time to clear the noise. You'll identify what actually matters in this season—and eliminate the obligations, roles, and distractions that don't align. From calendar clutter to emotional labor, this is where you reclaim your time, energy, and power.

This is where clarity becomes your filter—and your strategy.

> **Shift happens when you stop proving and start choosing.**
> Toni had always been the go-getter: promotions, new responsibilities, climbing the ladder as fast as possible. But after having two young children, that constant chase became suffocating. She felt stagnant and frustrated, like she was supposed to keep pushing but no longer had the energy or desire to do so. Once she anchored in her values, she realized this chapter of life called for something different. She gave herself permission to pause, to stay where she was, and to be fully present with her family—without guilt. Most important, she reframed "stagnation" as *strategy*. Her career wasn't over; she had a long runway ahead. She wasn't falling behind, she was building a foundation to soar when the time was right.

Ascend

With clarity and alignment in place, you're ready to move differently. This step is about protecting your energy, honoring your capacity, and directing it toward high-impact, high-alignment outcomes. You'll set firm boundaries, own your decisions, and expand your influence—without burning out.

This is where strategy meets self-worth—and real impact begins.

The Power of Saying No

When I walked out of that hospital, I made a decision: I would no longer waste my energy on things that didn't align with my deepest values. It wasn't just about cutting things from my schedule; it was about reclaiming my time, my focus, my life.

CHAPTER 8

Saying no is not about rejection. It's about *protection*. It's about choosing where your time and energy go. It's about ensuring that when you are present—whether in your career, with your family, or in your personal growth—you are fully there, not fragmented by a thousand unaligned obligations.

But for many women, saying no feels dangerous. It triggers guilt, fear, and a sense of failure. But the truth is, when you say yes to everything...you've just said no to yourself.

FROM EXHAUSTION TO INTENTIONAL LIVING

If you are constantly exhausted, stretched thin, or feeling resentful, it's not because you're failing; it's because your priorities are misaligned. The good news? You can shift. Right now.

Here's where to start:

1. **The Values Check:** Look at your current commitments. Do they align with what you truly value? If not, it's time to reassess.
2. **The Energy Audit:** For one week, track where your time and energy go. What drains you? What fuels you?
3. **The "Hell Yes" Rule:** If it's not a "hell yes!" it's a no. Begin practicing discernment with your commitments.

Identify Your Core Pillars

Before you can align your actions, you need to know what you're aligning *to*. That's where your core pillars come in—and they don't exist in a vacuum. They're grounded in your values.

Your *values* are the deep beliefs that define what matters to you. Your *pillars* are the containers—the life domains—where those values play out.

Think of it this way:
- If **freedom** is a value, maybe your pillar is *Career/Impact* because you crave autonomy in how you work.
- If **connection** is a value, maybe your pillar is *Family* or *Community*.
- If **growth** is a value, your pillar might be *Self*—your own evolution, healing, or leadership.

Values are the why. Pillars are the what.

When I refer to your core pillars throughout the Radical Prioritization matrix, I'm really talking about the values you want to protect and express across the most important areas of your life.

Your core pillars are the three or four unshakable areas of your life that matter most, the categories that, when nurtured, make you feel whole and grounded. Everything else is noise.

Think of your pillars as the framework for your decisions. Every yes, every no, every ounce of energy you spend should ladder up to these.

For most women, common pillars are:
- **Family:** Not just your role within the family, but your *relationships*—the ones that root you, stretch you, and remind you who you are beyond your titles. This pillar is about emotional connection, legacy, love, and the people you'd fight for without question.

- **Career/Impact:** Your contribution to the world, whether through a profession, a calling, or a mission. This is about doing work that matters—not just in output, but in *meaning*. It reflects your drive to lead, influence, innovate, and leave something behind that lasts.
- **Self:** The foundation beneath everything. This pillar includes your physical, emotional, and mental well-being—the part of you that gets neglected when you overfunction but holds the key to your capacity, clarity, and power. Without this, everything else cracks.
- **Faith/Spirituality:** Your connection to something greater—whether it's God, the universe, your intuition, or a personal code of belief. This pillar anchors you in purpose, helps you find meaning in the unknown, and provides direction when logic runs dry.
- **Community:** The relationships beyond your inner circle that fuel and challenge you. This is about belonging, connection, service, and shared growth. Whether it's giving back, showing up, or standing with others, this pillar reminds you that impact doesn't happen in isolation.

Keep in mind, you don't need a dozen core pillars. You need clarity on the top three or four.

How to Identify Your Core Pillars
Ask yourself:

- *What areas of my life matter most beyond the busyness, beyond the noise?*
- *If I stripped everything else away, what would I fiercely protect?*
- *Where do I feel most fulfilled when I invest my time and energy?*
- *What do I regret neglecting when I overextend myself?*

Write down your answers and then look for common themes. These are your pillars.

Your Priorities Should Ladder Up

Once you know your pillars, look at your calendar, your commitments, and your daily actions. If they don't ladder up to one of your core pillars, ask yourself: *Why am I doing this? Who am I doing it for? And what is it costing me?* (We'll dive deeper into this in a moment.)

When your priorities aren't aligned to your pillars, you end up exhausted and resentful. When they are aligned, you move with clarity, power, and peace.

KEY CONCEPT: ALLOSTATIC LOAD

The allostatic load is the accumulated wear and tear on the body caused by chronic stress and overwork. When women push through exhaustion for years without recovery, their nervous system remains in survival mode, leading to burnout, illness, and emotional depletion. You can keep carrying it all, or you can carry what matters. PowerShifters choose light, focused, intentional leadership.

Exercise
- Ask yourself: *Where am I hiding behind busy?*
- What's one area where you're overfunctioning?
- What simple (perhaps scary) action do you need to take instead?

The Radical Prioritization Matrix

When we're pulled in too many directions, we become distracted. We lose our power. We get scattered. But when we focus on what truly matters, we gain clarity and purpose.

There's a three-step process at the heart of Radical Prioritization:

Step 1: Anchor in Authenticity

The first step is reconnecting with who you are and what truly matters to you. Identify your core values—those principles that guide your decisions and define your mission. What drives you? What must you experience in your life? What excites you? This clarity will become your compass, helping you make decisions with confidence.

Step 2: Align Your Actions

Once you're clear on your values, it's time to align your actions with them. What truly matters? Where should you invest your time and energy? By focusing on the priorities that align with your values, distractions fade away. Intentional action leads to greater impact.

Step 3: Amplify Your Impact
Finally, it's about stepping fully into the impact you want to make. This is where your values and priorities come together to guide not only your personal life but also your contributions to the world. When you act with intention, your impact expands, creating a ripple effect that inspires others to do the same.

To help implement this, I created the *Radical Prioritization Matrix*—a visual tool that categorizes tasks, responsibilities, and desires according to alignment, priority, and potential impact. It's like a GPS for your life, helping you make decisions that are aligned with what truly matters.

How to Use the Radical Prioritization Matrix

The Radical Prioritization Matrix exists for one reason: to help you make aligned, high-impact decisions with clarity.

Most women are stuck in busyness, drowning in obligations, because they treat everything as equally urgent, equally important, and equally theirs to carry. This matrix forces you to stop that cycle. It challenges you to examine what's draining you, what deserves your energy, and what needs to go.

Here's how to use it:

CHAPTER 8

The Radical Prioritization® Matrix

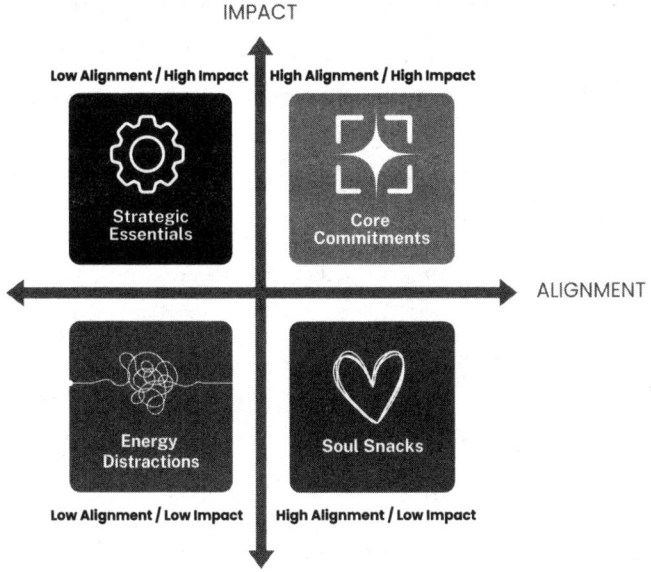

STRATEGIC ESSENTIALS
Low Alignment / High Impact: Streamline
- These actions have a large impact but are not aligned.
- If possible, delegate these to others or automate them.
- If you need to handle them, create efficient processes. Ensure they don't take too much focus away from aligned, impactful tasks.

ENERGY DISTRACTIONS
Low Alignment / Low Impact: Eliminate/Minimize
- These actions neither align with your values nor have a meaningful impact.
- These should be minimized, automated, or eliminated entirely.
- Ask yourself why you're doing these and consider dropping them. Keep them only if absolutely necessary.

CORE COMMITMENTS
High Alignment / High Impact: Focus
- These actions are both deeply aligned and have a significant long-term impact.
- These are your top priorities and should receive the majority of your energy. They lead to meaningful progress.
- Schedule these first. Build your daily routine around them.

SOUL SNACKS
High Alignment / Low Impact: Nurture
- These actions align with your values but have a smaller, more personal impact. They contribute to well-being, learning, and fulfillment but aren't as urgent.
- Treat these as self-care or personal development tasks. Integrate them as part of long-term growth strategies.
- Don't neglect these, as they nourish your personal growth. Keep them in your routine for balance.

Step 1: Brain Dump Without Censorship
Write down *everything* you're carrying: tasks, obligations, mental load items, random requests. Personal, professional...it doesn't matter. Don't filter. Don't justify. Dump it all on paper.

Step 2: Plot Each Item with Radical Honesty (and Zero Excuses)
This is where the real clarity happens. Look at each item from your brain dump and interrogate it—ruthlessly.

Quadrant 1: Strategic Essentials (Low Alignment / High Impact)

Anything that's necessary but draining belongs here. Ask yourself:

- *Does this matter for external impact (career, finances, team success), even if it's not fulfilling?*
- *Would dropping this have serious consequences for my business or family?*
- *Is this something that needs to get done, but not necessarily by me?*

Your job for these: automate, delegate, or limit the time it consumes.

Examples: *Quarterly reports, tax prep, certain meetings, administrative tasks, car maintenance.*

Quadrant 2: Core Commitments (High Alignment / High Impact)

For each thing you listed in step one, ask yourself:

- *Does this directly support my top five values and core pillars?*
- *If I do this consistently, will it move the needle in my life or career?*
- *Would future-me thank present-me for making this a priority?*

If your answer is a hell yes, it belongs here. These are your anchors. Protect them at all costs.

Examples: *Quality time with my kids, strategic leadership tasks, business growth activities, mental and physical health practices.*

Quadrant 3: Energy Drainers / Distractions
(Low Alignment / Low Impact)

This quadrant is where your time and energy go to die. Ask:

- *Am I doing this out of habit, guilt, or people-pleasing?*
- *If I stopped doing this, would anything meaningful suffer?*
- *Who is benefiting—and is it at my expense?*

Slash these aggressively.

Examples: *Scrolling social media, attending meetings that should've been emails, constantly "checking in," unnecessary errands, overvolunteering, overperfecting.*

Quadrant 4: Soul Snacks
(High Alignment / Low Impact)

Now let's determine your quiet power sources. Ask:

- *Does this light me up or restore me, even if it doesn't "move the needle"?*
- *Would skipping this leave me feeling depleted or disconnected from myself?*
- *Does this contribute to long-term resilience (mental, emotional, physical)?*

Stop treating these as optional. They sustain everything else.

Examples: *Reading, journaling, yoga, therapy, learning something new, creative hobbies.*

• • •

If there any items you're still not sure about, run them through this two-question filter:

1. *If I say yes to this, what am I saying no to?*
2. *Does doing this align with the woman I'm becoming or the one I'm trying to outgrow?*

If the answers make you squirm, it doesn't belong.

Step 3: Take Decisive Action

You've done the sorting. Now it's time to act. This isn't about tweaking your calendar; it's about owning your energy. Because awareness without action just keeps you stuck in the same cycle.

CHAPTER 8

Every quadrant tells a story. And now that you can see it clearly, it's your job to cut the noise, protect what matters, and move with ruthless clarity.

Here's how to lead from alignment:

1. **Core Commitments**: These are your nonnegotiables. Block time for them. Protect them.
   Build your week around these actions.
2. **Strategic Essentials**: Necessary but not fulfilling? Automate, delegate, or streamline.
   Handle them efficiently, but don't let them steal energy from your core commitments.
3. **Soul Snacks**: These are your *nurture* actions: soul care, growth, rest, reflection.
   They're not "nice to have"—they're essential to longevity and resilience. Schedule them intentionally or they'll get squeezed out.
4. **Energy Drainers/Distractions**: This quadrant is killing your bandwidth. Ask: *Why am I doing this? Who benefits?* Minimize, delegate, or eliminate these completely. If it's not aligned or impactful, it's stealing from what matters most.

Step 4: Make This a Ritual

This isn't a onetime exercise. Set a weekly time (perhaps Sunday nights or Monday mornings) to rerun your commitments through the matrix. If an energy drainer or distraction has crept back in, cut it. If your priorities have shifted, realign. When someone asks you to do something, run it through this

> **You don't need more time. You need more clarity.**

filter. Remember: You don't need more time. You need more clarity.

This tool isn't just for managing your schedule—it's how you protect your purpose. PowerShifters don't just fill calendars. They lead with precision. This is how you start. And how you stay aligned.

Less Doing, More Living

Radical Prioritization isn't about doing less for the sake of less; it's about making space for more of what actually matters. More peace. More purpose. More aligned success.

Because in the end, we don't remember the perfectly checked-off to-do lists. We remember the moments of meaning. The hands we held. The love we gave. The impact we created.

It's time to live like that—with radical clarity, intentional alignment, and the courage to choose what matters most.

YOUR POWERSHIFT STARTS NOW

Identify one commitment this week that does not align with your core values. Make a plan to either eliminate or delegate it.

1. Create a "priority filter"—a simple question to ask yourself before saying yes to anything new. Example: *Does this align with my long-term vision? Does this energize or drain me?*

CHAPTER 8

> 2. Set a firm boundary in one area of your life this week—whether it's protecting your time, energy, or focus.
>
> Radical clarity is not just about seeing what matters—it's about having the courage to act on it.

So I ask you: What does success look like for *you*? Not the version you've inherited, not the one you've been told you should want, but the version that feels true to who you are? Imagine a world where your energy is focused on what truly matters. A world where every decision you make aligns with your purpose. A world where your actions create meaningful impact.

It all begins with one shift—a radical act of prioritization.

That one decision has the power to realign your life and ripple into the lives of everyone around you. This isn't about doing less for the sake of it—it's about doing what matters most with unapologetic clarity.

PowerShifters don't settle. They choose with intention.

This isn't about doing less. It's about doing what matters most—on purpose.

CHAPTER 9

DO LESS. ACHIEVE MORE. AND STOP PLAYING SMALL

The more you let go, the louder your impact becomes. This is where you stop playing small. PowerShifters don't shrink—they expand.

It was supposed to be just another flight home. But halfway through the descent, the plane jolted so violently that most passengers gasped and clutched their armrests.

> **This is where you stop playing small. PowerShifters don't shrink—they expand.**

Lightning. We'd been hit.

For a moment, silence—thick, electric, suffocating. The kind of silence where fear takes up all the air. I sat frozen, staring out the window, every muscle locked.

Then it hit me: *What if this is it? What if I never make it home to my kids? What if they have to live without me?*

That moment cracked something inside me wide-open. I thought about the life I'd built—the constant hustle, the endless proving, the exhaustion I'd worn like armor. And I thought about what I'd leave behind: A mother always tired. A woman always doing, never being. A legacy of busyness instead of presence. I didn't want that. I couldn't pass that weight down.

The lightning didn't just strike the plane. It struck me awake.

> **True fulfillment isn't found in external accolades—it's found in impact.**

Some moments in life strip away the noise. They cut through the obligations, the distractions, the endless list of what feels urgent but isn't actually important. They leave you with terrifying clarity: *What am I really building? And will it matter when I'm gone?*

That was the moment I realized impact isn't what you do *someday*. It's what you choose *every day*. At some point in every high-achieving woman's journey, a pivotal question emerges:

What is all of this for?

We spend years—decades—climbing, proving, achieving. We hit the milestones, collect the titles, check the boxes. And yet for so many of us, an unsettling truth lingers beneath the surface: *It still doesn't feel like enough.*

Why? Because success without alignment leaves us feeling hollow. True fulfillment isn't found in external accolades—it's found in impact. Most people chase external success.

CHAPTER 9

PowerShifters chase internal alignment and let success follow.

This is where the shift happens: from personal achievement to meaningful contribution, from chasing success to creating significance.

KEY CONCEPT: THE GOLDEN CAGE

The Golden Cage is a metaphor for achieving a level of success that looks impressive on the outside but feels suffocating on the inside. Many women stay in careers or roles they've outgrown because walking away feels like losing everything they've worked for.

Is It Success or Performance?

Take a moment to reflect on your current role, title, or situation.

Answer these three prompts—quickly, without overthinking:

1. *What have I built that I'm afraid to walk away from?*
   (Be honest. Name the job, the role, the identity, the image.)
2. *What is it costing me to stay?*
   (Think energy, time, health, relationships, joy, self-respect.)
3. *If I weren't afraid, what would I choose instead?*
   (Don't justify it. Just name it.)

Now ask yourself: *Is this what I wanted—or just what I was told to want?*

The Frustration of Feeling Undervalued

Despite their ambition, intelligence, and contributions, many women feel unseen and undervalued in both professional and personal spaces. My research uncovered staggering statistics:

- 72 percent of women feel they are underpaid and earn less than they deserve.
- 57 percent are currently in, or have previously stayed in, a less-than-ideal relationship.
- 46 percent report feeling anxious frequently or very frequently.

These numbers aren't just data points—they reflect the exhaustion of generations of women who have poured themselves into systems that demand everything but give little in return. We're tired of working twice as hard to be noticed. We're tired of sacrificing ourselves for roles that don't see us. We're tired of waiting for permission to claim our impact.

> • • • •
> **Shift happens when you realize impact isn't given; it's claimed.**
> • • • •

The truth is, impact isn't something you wait for or something someone else defines for you. Too many women are waiting for permission, for someone to tell them what their impact should be. Stop waiting. Impact isn't granted. It's claimed by you, on your terms, in ways only *you* can lead. Shift happens when you realize impact isn't given; it's claimed.

CHAPTER 9

Impact Doesn't Mean Saving the World in Heels (Unless You Want To)

Many of us have been conditioned to believe that impact is something grand—something reserved for the people with big platforms, big influence, or big resources. But impact doesn't always look like a TED Talk or a bestselling book. Sometimes, it's holding the line in a meeting. Sometimes, it's saying no so someone else can step up.

Impact starts where we are.

- It's the way we lead in our careers.
- It's the way we raise our families.
- It's the way we show up for our communities.
- It's the way we honor our own worth, so others learn to honor theirs.

> **Shift happens when you stop chasing applause and start listening to yourself—even if what you hear changes everything.**
>
> Erin was the textbook high achiever—constantly chasing promotions, accolades, and external validation. She measured her worth by her LinkedIn profile and how often she could impress the audience in the room. But deep down, she felt disconnected and restless. She finally realized she had been chasing someone else's definition of success. She released the need to prove and started listening to what *she* wanted. The answer surprised her: She didn't want another title; she wanted to start a family. Once she stopped performing for approval and started aligning with her own values, she gave herself permission to make that choice. She didn't slow down; she shifted—toward a life that finally felt like hers.

Your impact isn't confined to your inbox. It shapes conversations, decisions, and culture across your organization. Impact is in the decisions you make, the people you affect, the conversations you lead, and the example you set—whether it's in a boardroom or around your kitchen table.

So the real question isn't, *Can I make an impact?* The question is, *What kind of impact do I want to make?*

CLARIFYING YOUR IMPACT: THE FIVE PATHWAYS

As women, our impact is multidimensional. To truly align our actions with purpose, we must determine where we want to create lasting change.

Here are the five key pathways to impact:

1. **Social Impact:** Creating change through activism, philanthropy, mentorship, and community leadership.
2. **Organizational Impact:** Transforming workplaces through leadership, innovation, and advocacy for equality.
3. **Familial Impact:** Redefining generational patterns and leading by example in personal relationships.
4. **Individual Impact:** Investing in personal healing, growth, and self-leadership to inspire others.
5. **Spiritual Impact:** Deepening your connection with purpose, values, and legacy beyond material success.

CHAPTER 9

> Which of these pathways speaks to you? Where does your heart pull you?

From Overextension to Focused Power

One of the biggest reasons women struggle to make a meaningful impact is because we are spread too thin. We are conditioned to believe we must do *everything for everyone*—but true impact isn't about being everything. It's about choosing where and how we want to make a difference.

This is where Radical Prioritization becomes key. When we stop diluting our energy across misaligned commitments, we amplify our influence. The clearer we are on our purpose, the more powerful our impact becomes.

So I ask: Can you feel the disconnect between who you think you are and who you're becoming?

Prioritize for Power: Own Your Influence

If you want to step into a life of true impact, start with these shifts:

- **Audit Your Current Influence:** Where are you already making an impact? Where are you pouring energy into things that don't align?
- **Define Your Legacy Vision:** If you could be remembered for one thing, what would it be? What kind of change do you want to contribute to?

- **Align Your Daily Actions:** Do your current commitments reflect the legacy you want to create? If not, what needs to shift?

Impact Isn't Big or Small—It's Intentional

The world doesn't need more exhausted, overextended women trying to prove their worth. It needs women who are clear, aligned, and unapologetically powerful in their purpose.

You are already enough. You don't need permission to step into your impact. You just need the courage to claim it. Is there an area of your life where you're holding back, waiting for permission to lead? What would shift if you stopped waiting? Impact isn't measured by title; it's measured by influence. Leaders who show up with clarity and alignment give teams permission to do the same.

THREE THINGS TO DO TODAY TO CREATE IMPACT

1. Identify one area where you want to create meaningful impact (social, organizational, familial, individual, or spiritual).
2. Eliminate one nonaligned obligation that is draining your energy.
3. Set a tangible goal in your chosen impact area. *(Examples: mentoring one woman, starting a passion project, advocating for change at work)*

Your impact begins the moment you decide it does.

CHAPTER 9

Burn Their Rulebook and Write Your Own

Success is not about what you achieve, but about the impact you make that is aligned with your purpose. So you've been chasing someone else's version of success? Well, now it's time to write your own.

We were taught that success looks like long hours, bigger titles, relentless productivity, and external validation. That the harder we push, the more worthy we become. That if we sacrifice just a little more, we'll finally feel like we've made it.

But let's be honest—how many of us actually feel successful? If success is supposed to feel fulfilling, why does it feel so empty?

The truth is, the version of success we were handed was built on depletion, not alignment. Success that costs you yourself isn't success at all. It's time to rewrite the definition.

A New Framework: Holistic Success

Success is not a title. It's not a salary. It's not the ability to juggle everything and never drop a ball. Success is alignment. It's fulfillment. It's impact that doesn't come at the cost of your well-being.

This is where *holistic success* comes in—a redefined approach that prioritizes

- well-being over burnout: Your success should support your health, not destroy it.
- fulfillment over obligation: If it drains you, it's not success—it's sacrifice.
- impact over overextension: Your legacy is built through intentional action, not endless busyness.

Holistic success is about designing a life that reflects what truly matters to you—not what's been imposed on you. Less hustling, more living.

It isn't about doing more—it's about doing what matters across every dimension of your life. It's the intentional integration of mind, body, heart, and soul, where clarity, vitality, connection, and purpose are aligned. In this model, success isn't just measured by external wins. It's felt internally in how alive, present, and fulfilled you are.

Your **mind** is where focus and growth live—your career, your finances, your goals. It craves challenge, clarity, and expansion.

Your **body** is your foundation—not something to push through, but something to honor. When it's fueled and supported, not depleted or ignored, everything else becomes more sustainable.

Your **heart** governs your relationships and emotional well-being. It asks for connection, intimacy, and presence—not performance.

And your **soul** is the anchor. Your values. Your why. The part of you that needs purpose and meaning—not metrics—to feel fulfilled.

> • • • •
> **Holistic success is about designing a life that reflects what truly matters to you—not what's been imposed on you.**
> • • • •

True holistic success follows a rhythm:

You *release* what no longer serves.
You *revitalize* your mind and body.

CHAPTER 9

You *restore* your heart and relationships.
And you *reconnect* with your soul's purpose.

That's not just a lifestyle shift. It's a PowerShift.

One of the biggest myths we've internalized is that doing more leads to greater success. But the women I've worked with—as well as my own journey—prove the opposite. When we do *less*, we actually achieve more—because what we do is finally aligned with who we are.

Success doesn't require proving, pushing, or burning out. It requires clarity, courage, and a willingness to let go of what no longer fits.

But please know, success is not static—it evolves with every season of life. We can't just redefine success once; we must consistently check in and realign as we grow.

HOLISTIC SUCCESS CHECK-IN

Ask yourself:
- *Does my current definition of success feel fulfilling? Or does it feel forced?*
- *Am I sacrificing my well-being for an outdated version of success?*
- *What do I need more of? What do I need less of?*

When we redefine success on our own terms, we stop living for the next milestone and start living for what truly matters.

Success, Reclaimed

The world tells us that success requires sacrifice. That rest is laziness. That enough is never really *enough*. But you know better now. Success is not about what you achieve—it's about how aligned you feel while achieving it. You don't have to prove your worth. You don't have to do it all. You are already enough.

So now it's time to build a life that reflects it.

Redefine Your Success

1. Write down your current definition of success. Does it align with what truly matters to you?

CHAPTER 9

2. What were you taught to believe?
3. How much of it still holds true?
4. What does success look like for you today? Five years from now?
5. What does it feel like?
6. How will you know when you've achieved it?
7. What do you want to hold on to? What do you want to release?
8. Define success in ten words or less without mentioning career or achievement. Read it daily for a week and notice how it changes your choices.

> • • • •
> **You don't have to prove your worth. You don't have to do it all. You are already enough.**
> • • • •

• • •

The world's definition of success is noise. PowerShifters define it in their own language—and live it out loud.

We're not here to fit into broken constructs. We are here to create new ones.

Your new success story starts now.

CHAPTER 10

THE RIPPLE EFFECT: ELEVATE YOURSELF, ELEVATE EVERYONE AROUND YOU

Your alignment isn't just personal, it's contagious. When you shift, everyone around you feels it.

When we think of leadership, we often picture CEOs, politicians, and public figures. But leadership is not about a title—it's about impact. The way you show up in your life doesn't just affect you. It influences your family, your workplace, your friendships, and your community. Your alignment—or lack of it—sets the tone for those around you.

Your choices speak louder than your words.

Think about it:

- When a mother learns to prioritize herself without guilt, her children learn that their needs matter too.
- When a leader values well-being over burnout, she creates a workplace culture that empowers others to do the same.

- When a woman demands to be heard and seen, she shows others they have permission to stand out.

The impact of one woman choosing Radical Prioritization doesn't stop with her—it creates a ripple effect that shifts entire systems. When leaders prioritize alignment over constant hustle, they don't just perform better; they model healthier success for their teams. They change cultures.

Growing up, many of us watched the women before us sacrifice their needs for the sake of others. We learned—whether consciously or not—that success meant overextending, that love meant self-abandonment, that strength meant suffering in silence.

Now we have a choice: Do we continue the cycle or do we break it?

When a woman steps into her own alignment, she unconsciously gives others permission to do the same. She becomes a role model not for self-sacrifice but for self-honor.

How Alignment Transforms Systems

When we shift from people-pleasing to purpose, from burnout to boundaries, from chronic doing to intentional being, the ripple effect spreads in all directions.

In Families

A mother who models self-care teaches her children that they don't have to earn rest.

A partner who communicates their needs creates a relationship built on mutual respect.

A daughter who sees her mother choose herself learns that self-worth is nonnegotiable.

In Workplaces
A leader who prioritizes work-life integration gives her team permission to do the same.

A manager who values aligned decision-making creates a culture of efficiency, not overwork.

A woman who advocates for herself paves the way for other women to step into their power.

In Friendships and Community
A friend who supports boundaries becomes a safe space for their friend's growth.

A community of aligned women shifts the cultural conversation from sacrifice to self-honoring success.

A movement of women leading in alignment changes the next generation's definition of success entirely.

Your Leadership Is in Your Living

The most powerful leaders are not the ones who tell others what to do. They are the ones who live in alignment with their truth—and in doing so, inspire others to do the same. The world needs more women who are so deeply aligned that their very presence shifts the spaces they enter.

So as you move forward on this journey, ask yourself:
- *What example am I setting for those around me?*
- *How is my alignment (or misalignment) impacting the people I love?*

- *What ripple effect do I want to create?*

Every choice you make in alignment creates ripples. You don't just shift for you—you shift for everyone who follows. When one woman chooses herself, she unknowingly gives thousands of others permission to do the same. And that? That is leadership. That's a PowerShifter.

BECOME A ROLE MODEL

1. **Identify One Area of Leadership:** Where in your life (work, family, relationships, community) can you be a role model for alignment?
2. **Set a Boundaries Challenge:** Choose one boundary you will reinforce this week and notice how others respond.
3. **Journal Prompt:** Reflect on a woman who has inspired you through her alignment. What can you learn from her?

We've Come So Far—but We Still Have a Long Way to Go

We've made undeniable progress.

Just a few generations ago, women couldn't vote, couldn't open bank accounts without a husband's signature, couldn't sit in boardrooms or call the shots. The women's rights movement cracked doors open that had been bolted shut for centuries.

CHAPTER 10

> **Shift happens when you drop what doesn't align and stop apologizing for it.**
>
> Priya was brilliant, hardworking, and reliable—but silent in meetings. She held back her thoughts and ideas out of fear: fear of judgment, fear of overstepping, fear of repercussions. Through applying the Radical Prioritization framework, she realized she was prioritizing safety over authenticity and impact. We worked on aligning her actions with her values: courage, integrity, and contribution. Slowly, she began speaking up, first in small moments, then in high-stakes conversations. The result? Not only did she gain respect and trust from her colleagues but she was awarded the company's annual Speak Up award, a recognition for those who model courageous communication and leadership. Her voice didn't just shift her career—it shifted the culture around her.

And yet, fifty years later, the gap between what's possible and what's expected remains staggering. Women still earn less than men on average. The majority of leadership, C-suite, and decision-making positions are still held by men (see https://www.equalpaytoday.org/gender-pay-gap-statistics/). And at home, the load is far from equal. Women continue to carry the invisible weight of household management, caregiving,

• • • •

When one woman chooses herself, she unknowingly gives thousands of others permission to do the same.

• • • •

social planning, and emotional labor, often while holding demanding professional roles.

The well-meaning message of "You can do anything" has quietly twisted into "You have to do everything." The result? A do-it-all generation of women stretched to the brink, quietly settling for imbalance and exhaustion because "that's just how it is."

But doing nothing—staying silent, staying complacent—is the fastest way to normalize and accept a standard that leaves us depleted and undervalued. The strain is real. The disparity is real. Waiting for someone else to fix it? I hate to break it to you, but no one is coming to save us.

It's on us—right here, right now—to shift this for ourselves and for our daughters.

Because they're watching. And what we settle for, they will inherit.

WHAT IS YOUR LEGACY?

The legacy you leave isn't built in the grand gestures. It's built in every aligned choice. That's what PowerShifters pass on.

Exercise

1. List three people who would be impacted if you chose to stop overgiving and start leading on your terms.
2. Write how you want them to describe you when they watch you live differently.

CHAPTER 10

> 3. Write a letter to your daughter, niece, or a young woman you mentor. Describe the life you hope she builds—then ask yourself if you're modeling it.

Why This Work Matters for Organizations

This book isn't just about personal transformation. It's about cultural transformation.

The Never-Enough Cycle doesn't just drain individual women; it quietly erodes teams, stalls innovation, and fuels disengagement. Burned-out leaders breed burned-out organizations. High-performing women operating from depletion eventually hit a wall—and when they do, so does the business.

But when women shift—when they choose alignment over busyness, impact over distraction, and purpose over proving—the ripple effect is undeniable. Meetings get shorter. Decisions get sharper. Teams become more empowered, more focused, and more resilient. Clarity scales.

PowerShifters don't just change their lives. They change cultures. They challenge outdated norms, dismantle toxic expectations, and model leadership that is clear, bold, and unapologetic.

If you're building teams, leading divisions, or shaping corporate culture, you can't afford to ignore this. The companies that will thrive in the next decade are the ones that make space for PowerShifters and encourage more women to become them. Because when women stop settling and start leading with radical clarity, they don't just elevate themselves. They elevate everyone around them.

And that's how organizations win.

Where Have You Been Playing Small (and Don't Even Know It)?

Challenging the status quo isn't just about big, headline-grabbing moments. It happens in the small, daily decisions, the ones you've been told are "just how it is."

In my national research study, women identified these key areas where they are settling:

- Salary
- Personal Health and Wellness
- Time for Personal Interests
- Overworking
- Personal Growth and Development

PowerShifters disrupt quietly before they disrupt loudly. The question isn't if you should challenge these norms—it's where you'll start. Here are some areas for you to consider:

Medical Care

Advocate fiercely. Women settle for dismissive care too often. If you feel unheard, ask again or find another provider. You deserve to be taken seriously.

CHAPTER 10

Household Labor
Stop quietly absorbing responsibilities. Start having uncomfortable conversations about division of labor and stop accepting imbalance as "normal."

PTA and Class Volunteer Roles
Ask yourself: *Why is it always the moms?* Challenge this by encouraging dads to step up—or openly decline and protect your bandwidth.

Overworking/Inability to Disconnect
Challenge cultures that reward burnout. End meetings on time. Be the one who logs off and normalizes it.

Working Hours and Remote Work
Advocate for flexible working hours and remote work options (where appropriate), emphasizing results over physical presence. This not only supports alignment but also enhances overall productivity.

Remember, when you live in alignment, you don't just transform your own life—you give others permission to do the same. Your daughters and sons. Your colleagues. Your friends, your partners, your community—they all feel the shifts you make. So the question is no longer, *Can I do this?* It is, *What happens if I don't?*

You've spent years carrying weight that was never yours—pleasing, performing, and hustling for approval.

But deep down, you already know: You don't have to do that anymore.

You are allowed to choose yourself. You are allowed to stop settling.

And when you do—when you stop shrinking, stop pleasing, and stop betraying yourself—everything shifts. Your light gets brighter. Your gifts become undeniable. And you give every woman watching you permission to do the same.

> **PowerShifters don't carry old stories. They see them. Thank them. Lay them down. And write new ones that are bold, unapologetic, and true.**

That weight you've carried? The stories that told you to play small and overperform? They were never yours to hold. It wasn't your fault. You were surviving in a world that demanded you disappear to fit. But survival is no longer the goal. Impact is. Freedom is. Alignment is. PowerShifters don't carry old stories. They see them. Thank them. Lay them down. And write new ones that are bold, unapologetic, and true.

This is your permission to release the weight, rewrite the rules, and lead without apology.

Remember, the world doesn't need more exhausted women proving their worth. It needs clear, aligned, fearless women who choose themselves and lead on their own terms. It needs *you*.

Every choice you make, every boundary you set, every action you take in alignment—it doesn't stop with you. It creates a ripple through your team, your organization, and your industry. When leaders choose clarity over chaos, their teams follow. When leaders model rest and intentional action, their organizations become more resilient. This is how you shift culture—not with policies and posters, but by leading differently.

So right here, right now, make that choice.

Stop settling. Own your voice. Bring your brilliance into the world without apology.

Because the life you want? The impact you're here to create? The legacy only you can leave? It all starts with one decision.

Shift doesn't stop with you. It multiplies.

THE END OF PROVING. THE START OF CHOOSING.

When I sat down to write *PowerShift*, it didn't feel as if I was simply pulling words out of my cognitive brain. It felt like something bigger was moving through me. As if all the moments—the crises, burnout, breakdowns, and breakthroughs—were pieces of a puzzle finally snapping into place.

This book isn't just a project. It's a calling. The message wasn't something I had to force; it poured through me as if it had been waiting all along. Sometimes your purpose doesn't whisper—it floods you. And when that happens, you don't just write it. You surrender to it.

I didn't just write this book for me. I wrote it for every woman who feels that same pull. For every woman who knows, deep down, that she's meant for more and is finally ready to stop carrying what doesn't belong to her, so she can rise into who she really is.

As we come to the end of this book, it's important to pause and reflect on the transformative journey you've just begun. Radical Prioritization is not just a strategy to better manage your time—it's a pathway to reconnect with who you truly are, to release the stories that no longer serve you, and to embrace the person you are becoming. It is not just about making your life easier, it's about making it truer. It's about stepping into a life where success is not defined by exhaustion, but by fulfillment. Where your worth is not measured by output, but by who you are at your core.

Reflect, Realign, and Reclaim

Throughout this book, we've explored deep questions of identity: *Who was I? Who am I? Who am I becoming?* These are the fundamental questions that have the power to shift the course of your life. By consistently reflecting on your identity and your values, you have the ability to intentionally align your life with the highest expression of yourself.

As you take the steps outlined below, I encourage you to reflect on these questions not just once, but continually—because life is ever-changing, and so is the person you are becoming. The work doesn't end here; in fact, this is just the beginning of a new chapter in your story, one that you write with intention, courage, and radical authenticity.

1. *Reflect on who you were.*
- What stories from your past have shaped who you are today?
- Are there old beliefs, identities, or patterns you are ready to release?
- How has your past informed the choices you've made, and how can you now make different choices that serve your true self?

THE END OF PROVING. THE START OF CHOOSING.

2. Realign with who you are.
- Who are you in this present moment?
- What values, passions, and commitments do you hold dear?
- How can you show up fully as yourself in your everyday life, regardless of the external noise?

3. Reclaim who you are becoming.
- Who is the version of yourself you are stepping into?
- What does your highest potential look like, and how can you prioritize actions that move you toward that vision?
- What legacy do you want to leave behind, and what daily practices will help you create that legacy?

Shift Everything. Choose Yourself. Lead Unapologetically.

The moment you choose yourself, the world adjusts. But it will fight you first. Choose anyway.

All the old versions of me were running from the same question: *Who am I?* The answer didn't come from doing more, carrying more, or proving more. It came from stopping long enough to ask, *What am I doing...and why?* And then having the courage to burn everything that wasn't mine to carry.

That's where freedom begins. Not in doing. In choosing.

PowerShifters choose.

They choose alignment.

They choose clarity.

They choose themselves.

Throughout this journey, we have uncovered the unspoken weight of the Never-Enough Cycle—the relentless pressure to do more, be more, and give more, even at the cost of our own well-being. We have explored the profound shifts that happen when we break free from external expectations and reclaim our time, energy, and purpose. We have dismantled the outdated definition of success and replaced it with one that honors our wholeness, our well-being, and our impact.

> **Radical Prioritization is about stepping into your fullest potential—not by doing more, but by being more of who you already are.**

Now the choice is yours.

Creating Sustainable Change: Your Radical Prioritization Action Plan

As I've mentioned, true transformation doesn't happen in a single moment—it happens in the small, intentional choices you make every day. Here's how you can take this work forward and integrate Radical Prioritization into your life for the long term.

Step 1: Commit to Clarity
- Revisit your values: What truly matters to you?
- Identify where you are still operating from obligation rather than alignment.
- Use the Radical Prioritization Matrix (from chapter 8) to assess where your time and energy are being spent.

THE END OF PROVING. THE START OF CHOOSING.

Step 2: Set Boundaries That Honor Your Worth
- Ask yourself: *Where do I need to start saying no?*
- What relationships, commitments, or expectations do you need to redefine?
- Write a personal boundary statement and say it out loud.

Step 3: Align Your Goals to Your True Impact
- What kind of legacy do you want to create?
- Where can you make the biggest difference in a way that feels fulfilling, not depleting?
- What small, consistent steps will move you toward that impact?

Step 4: Make Less Your Superpower
- Identify one thing you will stop doing immediately because it no longer serves you.
- Replace busywork with actions that fuel your purpose and joy.
- Simplify: If it doesn't align, energize, or fulfill, it doesn't belong.

Step 5: Build a Support System for Accountability
- Who in your life encourages and supports your alignment?
- Who do you need to set firmer boundaries with?
- Connect with like-minded women who are also choosing to live with Radical Prioritization.

THE RADICAL PRIORITIZATION CHECKLIST

- [ ] I have defined what success truly looks like for me (not society, not my workplace, not my family).
- [ ] I am aware of the pressures and expectations I need to unlearn to create more space for alignment.
- [ ] I am committed to saying no to what drains me and yes to what fulfills me.
- [ ] I have identified at least one boundary I will reinforce this week.
- [ ] I will celebrate progress, not perfection, on this journey.

The Power of Continuous Transformation

Remember, the process of Radical Prioritization is an ongoing one. As you evolve, so will your priorities and the ways in which you navigate the world. What you have learned here is not meant to be a onetime fix but rather a framework that supports you as you grow, expand, and continuously redefine what it means to live with intention.

Your identity is not a fixed state; it is a fluid, ever-evolving expression of who you are and who you are becoming. Life will throw you challenges, opportunities, and obstacles, but the power lies in how you respond—whether you choose to react from old patterns or create a new response grounded in your authentic self.

THE END OF PROVING. THE START OF CHOOSING.

So what happens next? You lead. You model being a PowerShifter. You stop settling and start showing the world what's possible.

Because the legacy you leave isn't about what you carry—it's about what you shift.

And shift happens right now.

You're not done. You're just getting started.

APPENDIX

•••••••••

RESOURCES FOR SUPPORT AND HEALING

If parts of this book stirred emotions or memories that feel heavy, please know you are not alone—and you do not need to carry it alone. Asking for help is not weakness. It's power. It's a decision to heal, to release old weight, and to lead yourself first.

If you've been hesitant to seek therapy or professional support, I understand. But please know this: The people who do this work—therapists, trauma specialists, mental health counselors, trauma-informed coaches—are some of the most caring, compassionate, purpose-driven professionals you will ever meet. They show up for this work because they believe in healing, in hope, and in helping others find their way back to themselves. You deserve that kind of support.

Following are trusted resources to guide you on that journey.

APPENDIX

Trauma and Mental Health Support
- **National Alliance on Mental Illness (NAMI)**—1-800-950-NAMI or nami.org
- **Crisis Text Line**—Text HOME to 741741 for free, 24/7 support
- **National Sexual Assault Hotline (RAINN)**—1-800-656-HOPE or rainn.org

Therapist Directory
- **Psychology Today's Therapist Finder**—psychologytoday.com/us/therapists

If You're Not Sure Where to Start

A simple conversation with your primary care provider or a local mental health center can be the first small step toward a big shift.

You deserve freedom, healing, and support. Choosing yourself includes knowing when to reach for a hand.

ACKNOWLEDGMENTS

To my girls: You are my heart, my why, and my greatest teachers. Everything I do, I do with the hope that you'll have a brighter future. May you always know your worth, speak your truth, and choose yourselves without apology. You are the legacy. And you are the future.

To the woman who's stood beside me not just in business, but in the trenches of growth: Thank you for bringing your love, strength, and grace into every conversation, every strategy, and every season of this journey. You've held the mirror up when I needed clarity and held space when I needed to fall apart. This work is sharper, deeper, and more aligned because of your presence in it. I am endlessly grateful for the power of doing this work with someone who leads with her whole heart.

To the women who came before me and broke through just enough of the system to make space for voices like mine: I see you, I thank you, I build from you.

To every woman who has read, listened, followed, worked with me, or shared her truth: Thank you. Your courage, your questions, your stories...they've shaped this work more than you know. You are the reason I write. You are the reason I keep showing up. This book exists because of you—and for you. Here's to your PowerShift. I'm honored to walk beside you.

This isn't the end.
It's the beginning of everything that's next.
Scan the code to unlock the next level:
Resources. Strategy. Support.
And access to a private circle for women who are ready to live and lead differently.
Your PowerShift starts now.

POWERSHIFT IN ORGANIZATIONS

A GUIDE FOR LEADERS, TEAMS, AND ERGS

When women stop performing success and start embodying it, organizations shift too.

PowerShift isn't just a personal framework—it's a leadership revolution. It's how high-achieving women reclaim clarity, capacity, and confidence. And when they do, entire systems rise with them.

Use *PowerShift* to spark meaningful dialogue inside your company, women's leadership network, or employee resource group.

Ways to Bring the Work to Life
- **Host a PowerShift seminar**—ignite honest conversation and catalyze strategic clarity across your women's leadership network or ERG.
- **Integrate Radical Prioritization** into your leadership programs to help women make aligned decisions that drive performance and fulfillment.

- **Build internal PowerShift Circles** to continue the conversation and embed the framework into daily leadership practices
- **Sponsor your female leaders to join The Shift Society**—the private community where ambitious women are redefining success.

Because when women are aligned, organizations are unstoppable.

Connect for Corporate Programs by contacting empower@gialacqua.com.

POWERSHIFT BOOK CLUB AND DISCUSSION GUIDE

GATHER. REFLECT. SHIFT.

PowerShift was designed to be experienced—not just read. When we reflect together, we amplify change. Use this guide to spark courageous conversation in your book club, leadership circle, or women's group.

Part I: The Cost of Performing Success
- Which part of the *Never-Enough Cycle* felt most familiar to you?
- Where do you see "busyness" showing up in your own life or workplace?
- What would *enough* look like if you defined it on your own terms?
- What's one belief about success you're ready to unlearn?

Part II: The Radical Redefinition of Success
- Which concept within *PowerShift* resonated most, and why?
- How has your definition of success evolved throughout the book?

- Which chapter or quote stopped you in your tracks—and why?
- What's one area where you're ready to trade guilt or fear for grounded power?

Part III: The PowerShift in Action
- What truth are you finally ready to say—to yourself or to someone else?
- How can you use *Radical Prioritization* to create more alignment in your life?
- What's one shift you'll commit to after finishing this book—even if it scares you?
- What was your biggest "aha" moment and what did it change for you?
- How will you use what you've learned to create a positive impact for others?